Hunger for experience

Hunger for Experience

VITAL RELIGIOUS COMMUNITIES IN AMERICA

John E. Biersdorf

A Crossroad Book
THE SEABURY PRESS · NEW YORK

The Seabury Press, Inc.
815 Second Avenue
New York, N.Y. 10017

Copyright © 1975 by The Seabury Press, Inc.

Designed by Carol Basen

Manufactured in the United States of America

LIBRARY OF CONGRESS CATALOGING IN PUBLICATION DATA

Biersdorf, John E   1930–
    Hunger for experience.

    "A Crossroad book."
    1. Religious communities—United States. 2. Religious and ecclesiastical insti-
tutions—United States. I. Title.
BL632.5.U5B53   200'.973   75–28079
ISBN 0–8164–1198–0

Contents

List of Tables   vii

Preface   xi

1. Hunger for Experience   1
2. The Modern Individuality Boom   12
3. Communities of Experience   34
4. Styles of Participation   60
5. The People Who Belong   83
6. Religious Vitality: Conservative and Liberal   97
7. The Challenge to the Liberal Churches   116
8. On Doing Something About It.   133

APPENDICES

A. *Groups that Participated in the Insearch Study*   141
B. *Insearch Conference Responses to Study*   163
C. *Conferees' Responses to the Study*   166

Notes   170

List of tables

    I. Groups Participating in the Study   38

   II. Organizational Activity   61

  III. Trust and Intimacy in Group Life   67

  IV. Interpersonal Values   67

    V. Personal Religious Discipline   72

  VI. Instrumental Values   88
Comparison of Members' Rankings with
Rankings of National Sample

 VII. Rankings of Concerns of Persons in Groups
with Concerns of General Population   90

VIII. Rankings of Fears of Persons in Groups
with Fears of General Population   91

  IX. Environmental Security Values of Members
of Insearch Groups   92

    X. Concerns for Social Order of Members of
Groups   95

  XI. Comparative Self-Ratings of Group
Members with Self-Ratings of General
Population   96

 XII. Conventional versus Individuated Values   102

XIII. Coherence of Group Categories According
to Valuing Patterns of their Members   122

To Margot

Preface

It began with a conference in Hudson, Wisconsin in October, 1969 on the "Relevance of Organized Religion." The issues raised in that meeting and the continuing interest of the George D. Dayton Foundation, which sponsored the original conference, resulted in the formation of a continuing committee to plan for the future. The members of that committee were: Dr. Colman Barry, OSB, Department of Religion, Catholic University, Washington, D. C.; John Dixon, Executive Director, Center for a Voluntary Society, Washington, D. C.; Rev. D. Alton M. Motter, Executive Director of the Minnesota Council of Churches, Minneapolis, Minnesota; Dr. James P. Shannon, Albuquerque, New Mexico; Rabbi Marc Tanenbaum, Director of the Interreligious Affairs Department of the American Jewish Committee, New York; Mrs. Cynthia C. Wedel, Associate Director of the Center for a Voluntary Society, Washington, D. C.; Dean Colin Williams, The Divinity School, Yale University, New Haven, Conn.; and Rev. Andrew J. Young, Jr., Atlanta, Georgia. The committee decided in late 1971, after much thought, to hold a second national conference to address this concern:

Churches and synagogues appear to be suffering a certain failure of nerve, while at the same time the longing for God and experimentation with religious forms are increasing. If this is so, the urgent need is not only for careful organizational planning, but for a vision, a creative image, within which planning makes sense. That was our hunch, and the conference was designed to nurture the formulation of such creative images.

The author, then the Executive Director of the Department of Ministry of the National Council of Churches, was called as project director; staff were recruited; and planning went forward for a conference to be held January 2–5, 1973, at the Cenacle in Chicago, Illinois. This book is based on the preparatory work for the conference, which was designed to give participants as much relevant background material as possible about current and predictable trends in the Judaeo-Christian religious traditions. That material included assessment of cultural trends, summaries of denominational statistics and social surveys of organized religion, and historical and theological reflections on the available data. Most preparatory time, however, was spent in a research study of creative religious communities which might be saying something about the future of religion. The preliminary findings of that study were reported at the conference and are more fully reported and interpreted in this volume. This book is published to make the research findings available to a wider audience, and to stimulate discussion and response to the challenges to organized religion that we believe were raised by the project.

The research, the conference, and this book are the combined efforts of many persons. I need first of all to express my gratitude to the George D. Dayton Foundation and its president, Wallace C. Dayton, for their generous support, and for the combination of freedom and helpful feedback by which they made the entire project possible. Yale Divinity School, through Dean Colin Williams, made computer facilities and faculty counsel available to us, and the Department of Ministry of the National

Council of Churches and its Board helped immeasurably by releasing staff for the project and providing office support, counsel, and encouragement. The Advisory Committee is responsible for the conceptualization of the project, for naming it "Insearch: The Future of Religion in America," and for planning and guiding it through its entire life. The cogency of the Committee's thinking and the accuracy of their intuitions and judgments about the current state of religion in American life were impressive and essential. I am particularly grateful to Priscilla Jones and Anne Tongren, who guided the research and conference planning stages consecutively, and to Don Archibald, who oversaw the computer work.

There is no space to list all of the researchers, coders, technical help, and conference staff, but I do want to express my personal appreciation to Paul Morton, Gerry Cook, and Phillip Garvin, who were responsible for the videotape and film presentations at the conference.

In the preparation of the book, I first want to thank Constant H. Jacquet, Jr., Colin W. Williams, and Martin E. Marty for their articles, which have contributed to my reflections on the research. My thanks also to Gwen Anderson, Laura Hembree, and Anne Tongren, who served as research assistants, and Marilyn Cook and Nancy Sellin for their careful and patient typing.

I hope that the book will be seen as an expression of a community of people who cared for each other in their varying commitments to a common task, and that it will encourage the formation and nurture the life of such communities.

                                        J.E.B.

1

Hunger for Experience

This land was settled primarily by immigrants who shared a book, who shared a story reaching back many centuries to a small Middle Eastern culture, and who believed that the living God of the story still revealed himself in love and judgment in the affairs of humans. The earliest settlers were Anglicans and Puritans, but they were joined by Roman Catholics, Lutherans, new varieties of Protestantism born in this country, Eastern Orthodox Christians, and Jews. The whole of the Judaeo-Christian tradition had played a major and complex part in American life. From the Mayflower Compact to the Declaration of Independence, from Lincoln's Second Inaugural Address to the leadership of Martin Luther King, Jr. in the civil rights movement, religion has justified public policy and shaped America's self-understanding. Judaeo-Christian traditions have been part of the personal lives of Americans as well—in the local church prominently positioned on the village green, in the bustling inner city immigrant parish, and in the excitement of the frontier revival meeting. The influence of this tradition has been pervasive in the rhetoric of politics and the law, and in the do's and dont's taught early in childhood. In short, these religious traditions have furnished a comprehensive meaning to integrate personal experience and order public life in America.

In contemporary American life, institutional religion seems to be stabilizing, or, according to some measures, declining while interest in informal experiential religion seems to be growing rapidly. General statistics on the current state of institutional religion indicate that, measured by membership and financial contribution, the long-term growth trend among religious bodies in this century is slowing down, and in some cases has even stopped and reversed.[1] (Statistics on the Jewish community are collected in such different ways that they cannot be usefully compared with data on Christian bodies.)

Church membership reported for all bodies in the U. S. has steadily risen since 1926 when a total of 54.6 million members was recorded by the *Census of Religious Bodies*. By 1955, total membership passed the 100 million mark and accounted for 61 percent of the population of the U. S. By 1960, recorded membership reached 114.4 million, 64 percent of the population. But figures compiled for 1970 indicated a total reported membership of 131 million, reflecting a one percent decline from 1960 in the percentage of Americans who are church members.

During the 1950s, the U. S. population increased roughly 20 percent, whereas recorded church membership increased from 86.8 million in 1950 to 114.4 million in 1960, an increase of 32 percent, exceeding the rate of growth of population by 12 percent. In the next decade, however, the growth of church membership and of the U. S. population were about even. This seems to indicate a slowdown of membership growth in the 1960s, especially in the latter part of the decade.

Statistics for membership growth among the denominations are very uneven, revealing highest growth rates among the Pentecostal bodies and other conservative groups, and lowest rates for the liberal Protestant denominations, four of which actually recorded lower membership in 1970 than in 1960: The American Baptist Church, the Episcopal Church, the United Church of Christ, the United Presbyterian Church in the USA.

Financial contributions to religious groups show a similar pattern. As the 1972 edition of *Giving USA* notes: "Religious institutions have probably been hurt most by inflation. Giving to religion the last three years gained 13.5 percent and represents a net loss to inflation of 2.5 percent."[2] In 1961, "religion" received roughly 50.5 percent of total philanthropic giving. By 1971 that percentage had declined by 10.2 percent. This trend is bound to have an important impact on the structure and viability of organized religion.

Not all religious bodies have felt the pinch of inflation equally, however. Per capita giving statistics over the past three years indicate that: (1) only Free Methodist Church contributions increased at a faster rate than inflation; (2) all the other religious bodies have been hit hard by inflation; (3) the "liberal" communions have been hit the hardest. The lower income groups, which are more prevalent in the smaller, conservative bodies, give a higher proportion of their income to church and other philanthropic causes than do those in the middle or upper income brackets, who make up the bulk of the four liberal communions. A recent study, *Punctured Preconceptions: What North American Christians Think About The Church,* lists the main obstacles to more adequate church support:

As people see it, the main thing blocking church support simply is a surpassing urge for more affluent living—for the "good things of life" that money can buy in the secular sphere apart from the church. This finding is in line with the general economic indicators, showing that the sharp upsurge in spending in other fields has more than doubled the rate of growth in support for the church. Rival attractions seem to be gaining more of the religious dollar. This suggests that the roots of church financial difficulties, at least in part, go far deeper than surface gusts about passing policies or programs, reflecting a shifting scale of values that tends to upgrade other interests more markedly over the needs of the church.[3]

The most dramatic recent development in religious life in this country, however, has been not the decline in institutional growth, but the sharp increase in interest in religion in the culture generally. The media, including both popular and scholarly literature, have widely reported this development, and what is most striking about it is its variety and range. Groups or movements experiencing tremendous growth in the last decade include: black religion, the Jesus Movement, the charismatics, transpersonal psychology, and the followers of Eastern disciplines.

These movements would seem to have little in common either theologically or sociologically. But one thing which characterizes them all is the search for, and reported rediscovery of, what is variously called "the presence of God," or "unitive consciousness." These movements all insist (to use Judaeo-Christian language) that one can experience the immediate presence of God, that such experience gives great joy and meaning to life, and that one's life can and should be guided by the presence of God. Even the transpersonal psychologists who study altered states of consciousness do so less as dispassionate value-free observers of interesting phenomena but more as seekers committed to personal disciplines which may change their lives. And charismatics find not only joy in their encounter with God, but also specific guidance for the problems of everyday life.

These developments are so widespread, and the single emphasis on religious experience in them is so strong that they cannot help but have a major impact on the faiths of the Judaeo-Christian heritage. We have called this phenomenon the resurgence of "religion of experience," and we believe it needs to be taken seriously by all concerned for the vitality of the Judaeo-Christian heritage in our changing culture.

The following two case studies provide very different examples of the contemporary concentration on religion of experience, one a lively Pentecostal church, the other an innovative liberal Protestant congregation.

King's Temple

King's Temple is an independent Pentecostal church in Seattle, Washington, which specializes in creative worship and particularly the use of music. There is a choir and an orchestra in its services. The pastor, Rev. Charlotte Baker, and the congregation believe that just as the Lord reveals spiritual languages or the gift of speaking in tongues, so he also reveals spiritual songs. As is the practice in some other Pentecostal churches, scriptural verses, set to familiar tunes, are sung in place of hymns. The visitor can easily follow the words in the Bible he or she should have brought along. The service is a remarkable freeform of alternating and complex rhythms of sung Bible verses, spiritual songs, and tunes by violinists, pianists, and other musicians into which the congregation flows with clapping, congregation-wide praying in tongues, prophecy, preaching, and healing. The worship is disciplined, orderly, and dramatic. The pastor is thinking about the introduction of dancing before the Lord. With characteristic carefulness and thought, members have prepared a position paper on the subject, and have held conversations on the topic for months while deciding whether to take action.

King's Temple began when the Rev. Charlotte Baker came to Seattle in 1963 and reopened a small unused church. As soon as she began holding services, she received from the Lord the promise: "Twelve months shalt thou labor, and then thou shalt see increase." Exactly a year from that date, over 100 people attended the Sunday service.

By August, 1969, the congregation had outgrown its small frame building and began construction of its present home. Building proceeded as money became available, and it is the proud claim of the congregation that, without going into debt or cutting mission giving, they completed the church by New Year's Day 1970, as promised by prophecy.

There are currently about 350 members of the congregation, which is primarily white, lower-middle- and middle-class, with some members who are well-off financially. People who had been suffering from alcoholism, drug problems, and emotional illness are constantly finding new life and deliverance in the church. In the group interview, one man referred to those who were "discards from society and those who are discards by choice" giving their lives to Christ and the church even though their worldly circumstances are comfortable. The church's vital worship and life are distinctive, as are the range of its mission activities and the commitment of its members. The twofold purpose of the group is to participate in the scriptural vision of the Glory of the Lord filling the earth, and to establish the believer in the local church—the house of deliverance and restoration. Specific goals express both sides of this purpose. The congregation has sent a missionary to Guam, maintains another missionary in Africa, and has recently instituted the King's Academy, a two-year seminary program for ministers and evangelists. King's Temple carries on prison ministries and youth programs, and has plans for a halfway house for young people. The congregation sends visiting teams to other churches, and looks forward to the time when it will be able to spend more money on mission than church maintenance. The pastor hopes that a segment of the earth will be revealed as a special concern for the church and its mission outreach.

Within the congregation, the emphasis is on the progressive revelation of God's truth to the members in new forms of worship, including communion and other rites, deliverance from demons, and new musical expressions. (And the pastor's wry admonition, "keep the church clean and pick up the junk.")

The language of the congregation mirrors the goals and indicates the rich symbols that have been developed from the Bible and liturgy to serve as a framework for group life: "seeking the face of God," "annointing of the Holy Spirit," "river of God," "Mt. Zion," "deliverance." One man remarked in the group interview, "There's one term you can't write down," and began speaking in tongues, to the great amusement of the rest of the group. After members receive the Baptism of the Holy Ghost, or spiritual language, speaking in tongues is under their conscious control. Praying in tongues is a recommended spiritual discipline.

King's Temple indicates the growth of the Pentecostal movement among the middle-class and well-educated people one would expect to find in a Presbyterian or other mainline Protestant church. Perhaps most significant is its attempt to take the doctrines of Providence and the Call seriously and literally. Members of King's Temple receive guidance in periodic presbytery meetings. God, through the laying on of hands, annoints prophets, who are recognized by the fellowship of autonomous congregations. A presbytery is led by prophets from other churches in the hope that they will stand apart, offering the Word of God, not their own opinions based on human knowledge. At the presbytery, members receive detailed instructions for the nature and direction of their ministry through the laying on of hands and prophetic utterances. The prophecies include assurance and general confirmation of faith as well as important specific instructions. Every office in the church, from teacher to Board member to pastor, is filled not by election or soliciting volunteers, but by prophecy. One either accepts the premise, or one does not. Either God calls men and women to ministry, or he does not. If he does, there ought to be some reasonable procedure for bringing together divine imperative, personal interest and ability, and mission opportunity. At a time when mainline Protestants are embarrassed by the concept of Calling, reinterpreting it in strictly secular terms as career planning, these revival Christians believe they know the way to ascertain God's call for their lives.

St. Francis Presbyterian Church

St. Francis Presbyterian Church, Fort Worth, Texas, is an intriguing combination of rigorous member discipline, liturgical renewal, human relations training and skills, and corporate social action in the community. In short, it seems to have appropriated most of the methodologies for church renewal available to mainstream Protestant denominations. They are effective in its task and vital in its group life. All that, and it is in suburbia, too. But the most important reason for including St. Francis may be its insistence on struggling through to a clear identity and purpose, in contrast to the style of those residential congregations which remain vaguely "pluralistic" in an attempt to satisfy many different needs and expectations. As the pastor wrote in a brochure on the 150-member church, "We do expect more from our people. And we are the first to say this situation may not be for everyone, but it is a dedicated attempt to restore meaning to being a part of the Church and bring meaning to the lives of persons who want it."

When the congregation was begun in 1965, the presbytery's committee wanted "something different than the prestige new church in suburbia," but evidently it did not know what that might be. During a series of initial retreats, members explored possible styles of organization and worship. As the church progressed toward official organization, members were encouraged to attend human relations labs, and by 1971, approximately eighty had participated in at least one such experience. One member said that the lab experiences had created a more open community. Through the lab experience members had developed skills in expressing themselves, dealing with conflict and making decisions. The church is committed to the use of consultants for training and decision making in the group's life.

A building fund-raising drive was held in the spring of 1968, but the effort to construct a multipurpose building to facilitate mission in the community was postponed because of rising building and finance costs. In the meantime, the church became preoccupied with the local Crisis in the Nation Program, which focused on the need for child care facilities for blacks in the community. In 1969–70, a "year of agony," the congregation finally voted to postpone the building in favor of engaging in a process to clarify the purpose and goals of the church. According to the group interview, those members who had had human relations experiences became less interested in the building and more concerned with personal values.

About one-third of the members of St. Francis left during this year of conflict, which resulted in the decision not to build but to be a house church using leased space. Those who remained experienced an increasing sense of common identity as they addressed the question, "If we don't want a building, what do we want?" By November, 1970, when a meeting was held to articulate the church's goals, the issues seem to have been resolved. The purpose of the group was stated in the group interview: "To develop power within each one of us according to our potential as God's creation and then to reach out beyond ourselves in risk to challenge structures in a continuing process."

Strategies for attaining that purpose include: continuing enrichment in nurture groups, informing the group of needs in the outer community, helping people to identify their own talents and skills, launching mission groups into the community around specific issues, and developing support systems to sustain members in the bruising task of mission. Considerable stress is placed on the church as a pathfinder, and an innovator and experimenter in mission and in its own life. Among the several metaphors persons used to describe St. Francis is that of an emergency room. The members see their mission as acting in an emergency and carrying through with the healing process.

Two characteristics of St. Francis church stood out strikingly in the group interview. The first is the thorough skill development of members in group process and human relations training. One senses a mature group able to deal with both feelings and tasks, to listen to each other and work through difficult decisions. The applied behavioral sciences appear to offer genuine and powerful aids to mission and church renewal in this congregation.

The second striking characteristic is the commitment of the church to social action in the community. One new member mentioned continually meeting people from St. Francis in decision-making and political activities in the community. He was amazed to find so many people from such a small church so active in community affairs; in his former 2500-member church, he had never met anyone, "except passing the plate on Sunday morning." The church's style primarily consists of individual actions supported by group nurture rather than corporate action as such. However, mission groups have engaged in community action not, as one member remarked, as "a little social action committee," but as an integral part of the church's total life.

King's Temple and St. Francis Presbyterian Church exemplify the resurgence of religion of experience. In the following chapters we will define and analyze religion of experience, illustrating it from the groups in the study, and we will suggest what religion of experience implies for the future of institutional religion.

As in the cases of King's Temple and St. Francis Presbyterian Church, religion of experience can transform human lives for good. But issues can be raised about religion of experience. A religion of experience can tend to be a religion of emotion—leaving one with a certitude about all one's prejudices and vested interests, and a frightening drive to impose them on one's fellows—for their own good. It may also be elitist and perfectionist—striving after certain special experiences and granting status to those who achieve them, while judging as spiritually "tone deaf" those who do not. A religion of experience can become a religion of *private* experience, encouraging personal comfort at the expense of concern about one's neighbor, cutting the nerve of conscience that judges every spiritual gift according to its fruits.

Whether for good or ill, the religion of experience is here to stay. This book argues that the mainstream religious institutions of the Judaeo-Christian tradition must come to terms with it, for the sake of their own mission and life. In a time of change, and in a pluralistic culture, people will seek for meaning to meet their needs for identity, power and personal relationships. They will seek this meaning in church or synagogue, in education, in encounter groups, in the arts, or wherever they can find it. The church and synagogue purport to carry a gospel proclaiming that God is with us, bestowing by his grace, personhood, power and relationship. Religion of experience insists that the claim must be tested—by experience.

This book is a report on a research study of vital religious communities in America. It offers some empirical data and some reflections on their meaning for those concerned about the future of church and synagogue in our society. "Hunger for experience" was found to be descriptive of the growing edge of religion in American life. Historically, religion in American culture has always emphasized experience, but the pluralism and change of contemporary life seems to reinforce the need for it.

Chapter two describes those aspects of contemporary life which increase the demand for a "religion of experience." Chapter three describes the process by which groups at the "growing tip" of religion were identified for study, and some basic themes common to groups from diverse theological and denominational backgrounds. In chapter four, three basic styles of participation in religious life are identified and in chapter five we examine findings about members of the groups chosen for the study. Chapter six looks at the criteria by which religious vitality may be assessed, and the final two chapters point to implications of the study for those concerned to revitalize contemporary churches and synagogues.

2

The Modern Individuality Boom

WHY A RELIGION OF EXPERIENCE?

Religion of experience is not a sudden development on the American scene. In some ways, religion in America has *always* been a religion of experience. If this quest for experience has intensified, as we believe it has, it is because of the increasing amount of pluralism and the accelerating rate of social change that Americans are now experiencing.

Pluralism

No religious belief system or myth can encompass all of life in the modern world, and no religious institution can serve more than part of a society. We are used to that insight, calling it the acceptance of pluralism. But pluralism seems almost too gentle a word to describe the fragmentation, confusion, and meaninglessness that characterize contemporary culture. Contemporary pluralism results in a need for authentic and powerful experience to give meaning to personal life and to integrate the social order. In modern society people need meaning-laden, integrating experiences. They live their lives relating to institutions which have no necessary relationship with each other, which share no common myths or values. The company for which a woman works, for example, is concerned only about those aspects of her self that contribute or do not contribute to her performance on the job. Her non–job related skills, ambitions, and interests are of no concern to the official structures, although she may find informal friendships at work. In a more traditional society life was more of a whole. A man was willing to work long hours at a routine job because economic necessity demanded it. In addition, major and secondary institutions and common opinion all approved work as a responsible and worthwhile way to spend a major part of one's life. Common sense, or "what everyone knows," was the guide to everyday living and basic values. It even linked one's different social roles in a coherent myth that gave purpose to life.[1] But common sense in modern life seems fragmented, confused, and even contradictory.

To understand the pluralism of contemporary culture then, we need first to understand the function of religion as "myth," and the changes in religious myth over the centuries.

The various faiths of the Judaeo-Christian tradition constitute a fundamental context or metaphor for approaching life. Just as a certain picture of reality furnishes the basis for a scientific tradition and community, guiding the formulation of hypotheses and the development of methodologies to test them, so the Judaeo-Christian picture of reality means to guide one's understanding of life, and how one acts, especially in relation to fellow human beings. It is customary to call such general belief systems "myths." Myths are very general descriptions of reality, but they are not sets of abstract propositions from which one can deduct concrete statements about specific situations.

A myth serves at least two purposes—it helps us gain power over ourselves and over the world in which we live; and equally essential, it makes sense, giving meaning to our actions, our participation in community life, and our self-identity. Myths or beliefs reside in the tradition of communities. One absorbs the myth by learning to live and function in the community. It is important to remember that the skills, beliefs, and feelings which express the myth are usually not taught at the conscious, cognitive level. It is not possible to succeed in business without really trying, nor to believe with one's whole heart in the Lord Jesus Christ by simply consulting a manual and learning the answer. As Michael Polanyi wrote, "We know more than we can tell."[2] We learn the myth at *all* levels of our being, not just the cognitive, and it is by means of the myth that we understand ourselves and act in our world.

The word "myth" has another connotation in common language: something that is not really true, or that is only figuratively true. That connotation is itself an expression of modern sophistication. The idea that one can stand outside of oneself, as it were, and examine the fundamental beliefs by which one lives one's life (i.e., one's myth) was unknown in earlier times. Primitive people, according to Durkheim, had no such critical distance from their myth. In fact, they did not even know they had a myth. Their society itself was the myth, fully articulated to form and guide all of human life.[3] The idea that a myth may be only partially true is the product of modern civilization with its differentiation of society into separate institutions, each with its own responsibility for one area of life.

Thomas Luckmann has traced the historical differentiation of myth in Western civilization from its full articulation in societal life to its becoming a property of specialized institutions called churches and synagogues.[4] As Western society became increasingly complex, specialized institutions arose to assume responsibilities for various areas of the common life. Religious organizations became the custodians of what Luckmann and Peter Berger call the "sacred cosmos," preserving and elaborating it, and teaching it to each new generation.⁵ But the sacred cosmos now became the property of a special organization, whose specialists were removed from the common daily life of much of the community. Consequently the impact of religious traditions in such realms as the political or economic diminished, and religion was now at a distance from the pressures and demands on the life of the individual.

Medieval Catholicism dealt with this problem by means of two very different strategies—one from above and one from below. From above, the Church attempted to extend its corporate power over other institutions in order to enforce the presence of its myth throughout society, hoping to establish a New Israel as homogeneous as the old. From below, St. Francis and his spiritual brothers and sisters attempted to live a unified personal life, totally devoted to God in all its aspects. As Jesus called his disciples one by one into a new life, so latter day Christians ought, through voluntary choice and the grace of God, to be brought one by one into the Kingdom.

A few centuries later, the United States dealt with the problem of isolation of the religious myth by official reliance on the second strategy. The authors of the Constitution were mindful of the varieties of religious traditions that came to these shores. They were also wary of the subtle ways in which the Church's zeal to extend the sacred cosmos becomes a zeal to enhance its own corporate power, made more tyrannical by the claim that opposition to its power is sin against God and his truth. (This is an instance of what Luckmann refers to as the "secondary functions" which religious organizations develop to maintain and enhance their institutional life and corporate power, and which make their claims to represent the sacred cosmos less credible.[6]) By inserting the separation of church and state into the Constitution, the authors established the principle of voluntarism in relation to the religious myth. One had to *choose* the religious myth consciously in its Methodist or Baptist or other form, aware that there were adherents of alternative forms of belief in the same town, who held their version with equal certitude. Or if one was a Lutheran because all Swedes are Lutherans, the sacred cosmos was simply the property of one subculture in a land of subcultures.

Thus, by a fundamental and deliberate political decision, religion in America became a *voluntary* religion. Religious organizations, therefore, had to respond to the increasing pluralism of modern times by strategies of individual persuasion building up *voluntary* associations to proclaim the faith. As Winthrop Hudson points out, in contrast to the state-supported parishes of the Old World, in America, "a . . . new beginning had to be made by individual clergymen recruiting their own congregations out of a population that was largely unchurched."[7] From the beginning, American churches and synagogues have been voluntary associations, typically democratic in nature even when official doctrine holds otherwise. They have been forced to be adaptive to cultural, social, and economic influences, and must hold laity in high importance as they continually renegotiate their existence on the basis of the felt importance of the services they offer.

In addition to the voluntarism and diversity that have historically characterized American religion, there has been an optimism about the possibilities of thoroughgoing reform and an experimentalism. Looking back over their brief history in New England, Increase Mather declared in 1677 that "there never was a generation that did so perfectly shake off the dust of Babylon . . . as the first generation of Christians that came to this land for the Gospel's sake."[8] The desire for and optimism about reform issued in a desire to humanize the whole social order. American insistence on testing doctrine and authority by personal experience led, at its worst, to a preoccupation with methods and techniques. This, in conjunction with the diversity of American religious traditions, precluded a uniformity of belief and organization.

As voluntary associations in a pluralistic culture, religious institutions evolve as they attempt to proclaim their message to a changing society. Thomas O'Dea has described the dilemmas which face every religious movement. The group must institutionalize to make its message available to later generations,[9] but in doing so, it inevitably distòrts the original intentions of its message and makes reformation necessary. The message of the religious movement and the ritual in which it is set must be standardized and objectified in order to reflect the original experience faithfully. But when this happens, the message may become alienated from the personal subjective experiences of participants. The myth must be related to the preoccupations of daily life, but in the process, it may become trivialized into mere regulations for daily activities instead of a call to a new life.

The dilemmas of the religious movement continue. The organization that carries the message must establish administrative procedures and structures for organizing community life, but in so doing it may spawn a cumbersome bureaucracy unresponsive to changing conditions. The organization must become powerful enough to survive amidst other myth-bearing communities, but it may become more preoccupied with enhancing its own power than with the message. And finally, to survive through time, the myth and the community must appeal to a variety of self-interests among the members, which will inevitably distort the more single-minded intentions of the founders to live a life governed only by the new reality they have experienced. So the institutions that are intended to preserve the revelatory events and make them available for future generations inevitably themselves become obstacles to that revelation, and must in time be challenged and transformed. The rhythm of creation, redemption, and new creation, which is a central concept of the Judaeo-Christian myth, is also a sociological principle of the evolution of the religious myth and the institutions that carry it.

Change

Ours is not only a pluralistic culture, but one where the rate of change is accelerating. The shape of religion in America is determined by that fact. Futurologist Alvin Toffler, documents the increasing change caused by the advance of science and technology.[10] The time lag between the invention of a new idea, its application, its diffusion to a mass market, and the feedback of another new idea is constantly decreasing. In the coming future things, people, places, organizations, and ideas are all more transient. Things and ideas become obsolete faster. People are more mobile geographically, and relationships and organizational affiliations shift more rapidly. The combination of acceleration and transience produces a third characteristic —novelty. Toffler holds that there are identifiable psychological and physiological maladies that can be called "future shock," which result from a person being exposed to more novelty than he can deal with. Symptoms of future shock include unreasoning hostility to authority, violence, apathy, erratic swings in lifestyle, and withdrawal.

It is difficult without much more research to know how applicable this general picture is to the various subcultures in American society. Toffler estimates that perhaps seventy percent of Americans still live in pre-industrial society.[11] About twenty-five percent live in the latter stages of industrial society, and perhaps two or three percent in various pockets in government, aerospace, and the university live now in post-industrial society. But these two or three percent are facing now the problems that an increasing number of the population will face in the future.

THE MODERN INDIVIDUALITY BOOM

Pluralism and continuing change, so characteristic of modern society, have serious implications for the living of one's personal life. Thomas Luckmann compares people in modern society to consumers in a supermarket: picking their values by personal choice according to their various social roles and life involvements, and putting them together in a privatized individual myth which is a shaky support for life because it has no enduring institutional base.[12] This personal construction of myths caused by the rapid change and consequent fragmentation of modern life is good news to some people but bad news to others. For those who have been trapped in a family or small town that has no place for their interests or personality traits, the freedom or diversity of the large city is cause for celebration. Such people welcome a culture which takes on more and more of the characteristics of metropolis. For those who have been oppressed because of race, color, sex, or socio-economic origins, continuing institutional change offers the hope of overcoming oppressive structures. But for those who have received their myth from stable institutions buttressed by friendships and family, continuing change is upsetting and threatening. And for those already so bewildered by the fragmentation and conflict of values in modern society that they are unable to form a stable personal identity, the challenge to construct their own myths can be devastating.

To the always problematic task of being human, the modern world imposes on each of us an additional burden of responsibility for our own identity and meaning. Saul Bellow's Mr. Sammler muses about the achievement of Western civilization in asking each person to be an individual, responsible for his own life myth, instead of being a member of the social order, receiving his personhood from the church, the state, the family, the tribe, the race. Mr. Sammler worries about "The Modern Individuality Boom." "This too great demand upon human consciousness and human capacities has overtaxed human endurance. I am not speaking only of moral demand, but also of the demand upon the imagination to produce a human figure of adequate stature. What is the true stature of a human being?"[13]

Our study examined a great variety of religious responses to the burden of imagining and producing a separate self. But we need to note the difficulties of the synthetic task that faces the consumer in the supermarket of values. The symbolic canopy of a traditional religion had a sturdiness about it. It was the creative interactive achievement of generations, adapted to all the expectable life crises and situations, and it had been tested and refined in the daily lives of millions of people. One could safely fit one's life into it, knowing that there would be sound guidance for all that life might bring, as well as some room for the expression of one's idiosyncracies. But in the modern world, where the religious tradition represents only one set of values, and where there is so much change that no tradition can anticipate it, it is a profoundly difficult task to construct a personal life myth out of the available resources. People often take a partial belief and attempt to stretch it to meet needs it was never intended to meet. Erik Erikson suggests that this attempt is due to the fact that "neurotic patients and panicky people in general are so starved for beliefs that they will frantically spread among the unbelievers what are often as yet quite shaky convictions."[14] So encounter groups, psychoanalysis, or political beliefs may be made to serve as a whole world view.

The Need for Experience

Alvin Toffler has pointed out that the product increasingly offered by institutions to consumers in contemporary society is not goods or services, but experiences.[15] The United States is the first country in history in which services account for more of the gross national product than manufactured goods. But Toffler sees a further movement beyond goods and services toward the furnishing of experiences, which will in time become the dominant sector of the economy. Admittedly, the distinction between experiences and services or even goods is not always clear cut. A flight from New York to San Francisco is a service. But friendly, attractively dressed stewardesses, a film, music, drinks, and meals and snacks in varying degrees of culinary quality all suggest that what is being merchandised as much as the transportation to the other coast is a pleasant and enjoyable experience en route which will hopefully induce the traveler to choose this airline over another the next time.

People in modern society *consume* experiences and meanings, choosing between meaning symbols as consumers choose products in the economic marketplace. Television commercials suggest peculiar relationships between personal hygiene habits and sexual fulfillment, and the printed media offer different mythic perspectives on national events. As a result, human life is compartmentalized and privatized. People are left to their own resources to put together their various social roles into a coherent self. In short, each person must create his or her own myth.

These circumstances make what Luckmann calls "secondary institutions" especially valuable.[16] The privatized person in industrial society needs voluntary groups—churches, synagogues, service organizations, or even recreational clubs—in which he or she can relate as more than a consumer or worker, in which the total person can draw together the various social roles into a coherent and meaningful self-identity. Friends are also necessary for personal integration and continuity of self-identity, especially if the network of friendships endures throughout the life span and connects across the generations. And finally, of course, the family takes on added burdens. The nuclear family of parents and children must carry financial and management responsibilities and simultaneously must satisfy needs for mutual support, friendship, and nurture. However, the high divorce rate indicates that it is difficult to sustain the stress of these responsibilities over a long period of time. Consequently, the family unit dissolves and may or may not be formed again after much pain and loss.

Religious organizations are only one of the many secondary institutions in American culture that are responding to the modern individuality boom by offering meaning-laden experiences. Alvin Gouldner found that twenty-seven percent of the sociologists attending a national convention at one time had intended to become ministers, priests or rabbis.[17] Gouldner suggests that this is evidence that in contemporary society the social sciences have adopted a function similar to religious institutions—that of furnishing meaning and values for living in the modern world. He points out that much of the research in the social sciences has not been aimed at discovering new knowledge, but rather furnishing meaning in a changing time. The social sciences have also adopted such functions of organized religion as reducing the dissonance between what we think and feel, providing orientation in the society in which we live, and generating order in the world. Besides the churches, synagogues, and now the social sciences, such other institutions in contemporary society as the university, the mental health professions, the media, and even leisure-time organizations serve as important "meaning makers."[18]

WHAT IS RELIGION OF EXPERIENCE?

The combined factors of pluralism and change in contemporary American culture have given rise to the modern individuality boom. In response to that boom and the loss of meaning it represents, secondary institutions offer integrating, meaning-laden experiences. Churches and synagogues are only one type of secondary institution, and they face sophisticated competition from the others in attempting to meet the same needs. But people still look to religious institutions for meaning-laden experiences. Deep in the American religious consciousness, from the Great Awakening in 1740 until now, there has been the conviction that doctrine and authority must always be tested on the ground of experience. In the intemperate words of Gilbert Tennent's sermon in 1740, "Is a blind man fit to be a guide? . . . Is a dead man fit to bring others to life? . . . Isn't an unconverted minister like a man who would learn others to swim before he has learned it himself, and so is drowned in the act and dies like a fool?" When the culture is swamped by confusion and change, those who seek new strength and direction will return to that bedrock conviction, not simply because it is in the past, but because it is the best way we know to live the gospel of love.

Religion of experience takes many different forms, as we will see. For some it means the security of traditional beliefs and forms. For others it means discarding old religious ideas and institutions, and seeking among the social sciences and Eastern religions for new techniques, judged in the crucible of personal experience. For most, however, religion of experience is found less and less in the traditional, stereotyped patterns of religious activity because of competition from increasingly sophisticated, secular, meaning-making institutions. For growing numbers of people, the search for a religion of experience leads to diverse meaning-making communities that can offer the intimacy of interpersonal relationships and authentic personal religious experiences and disciplines.

Religious communities in America have always been voluntary organizations, communicating their myths to the surrounding culture by means of powerful meaning-laden experiences. The dominant strain in American religion historically has been experience, not creed or church membership. When a culture becomes fragmented and confused, as is ours, people hunger for experiences to help them integrate their lives and find strength for living. Our hypothesis in this study was that those churches and synagogues which respond to this hunger for experience would be judged especially effective by religious leaders. To test this hypothesis, we first needed to agree on what an experience is.

Experience

An experience, first of all, connects inner and outer reality. To use the most hackneyed of examples, the experience of viewing a beautiful sunset or scenic vista is moving precisely because the external reality elicits a profound and complex inner emotional response. In addition to touching our inner life, an experience has an intrinsic value. It is a worthwhile event for its own sake, not because it is a means to another end. Time spent with one's beloved is not useful for something else; the very suggestion is abhorrent.

An experience is often new, unique, or renewing. The experience of watching and hearing and smelling the active volcano on the island of Hawaii was important for me precisely because it was the first time I had experienced the earth opening and molten rock crashing and flowing out. But an often repeated event can also be a renewing experience when it surprises a habitual perception and increases love or vision; as, for example, in talking with a child over a routine matter and suddenly being struck afresh by the child's vitality and beauty.

In addition an experience is essentially connected with meaning. The great mystical experiences leave a residue of meaning or myth behind. They are often paradigmatic events which make sense out of the other events in life. So powerful are these mystical experiences that they demand the transformation of one's understanding of reality in order to establish their truth. Let me explain this in more detail. An experience and the interpretation given to it are separable only in thought. I can see another person only because I have a preexisting perceptual model of a person that enables me to make sense out of the light and dark patches I see. And I can act on what I see only because I possess some interpretive schema based on my under-standing of past experience that enables me to conceive a goal and act in ways that lead to that goal. We use such perceptual and action schemas every day. An important experience, such as the mystical experiences described above, challenges our habitual schemas to take the new event into account. When the schema adjusts to include the new experience, the schema is changed. As the *trans-formed* schema is brought back into habitual use, our everyday living is changed.

Important experiences touch many areas of life in an interconnected way, and the new meanings which grow from them are often at the fundamental level of myth; that is, they have to do with one's personal identity and one's connectedness with other human beings, the earth, and God. New meanings at such a level are often difficult to articulate. Gerald and Elizabeth Jud have developed the Shalom retreats, which focus on marital relationships us-ing norms derived from a New Testament understanding of *agape* and methods from the contemporary human potential movement. At the close of the retreat, participants are asked to write about their experiences. The result is often a reclaiming of traditional Christian language, which was learned in Sunday school but since discarded. After the retreat experience the language has meaning; it is the only or the best way to articulate the new reality.[19] Another frequent consequence of a powerful experience is the opposite reaction, namely that *no* words can be found to describe the changes that have taken place. "There's no possible way to describe it, you'll just have to experience it yourself," is an especially frustrating message for the non-initiate. But both the loss of words and the new affirmation of traditional words indicate that the experience has broken the old meaning system. Some profound change has taken place within the person because of the experience, and in time a new perspective on life, a transformed myth will arise.

A final characteristic of important experiences has already been implied. They often grant power to the one having the experience. Important experiences can profoundly stir the emotions and touch conscious and unconscious levels of personality. When the effect is personally confirming, the residue can be a sense of personal power, peace, and joy, which may last into the days and weeks following. If the experience has touched levels of anger, pain, or fear in such a way as to integrate them with the rest of the personality, a changed and more confident self may gradually emerge afterward. Important experiences have such power that people tend to remember their personal histories in terms of such events. These experiences then order the rest of their lives into meaningful narratives.

Experiences, of course, range from unimportant to important. What distinguishes an experience from the automatic routines of daily living is that it occasions some transformation of ordinary perceptions and habitual activities. An important experience causes a person to change his routines to respond to the event. Even so, experiences may be as modest as seeing a leaf in a fresh new way or as self-transforming as falling in love. Experiences may be spontaneous, or they may be intentionally planned by institutions and intentionally sought by persons. Institutions cannot guarantee that their careful preparations will result in an experience for any one person, but they construct environments with the hope that such experiences will result. Likewise, people contract to participate in certain activities with the same expectation. A person may shop carefully before deciding whether this encounter group, that skiing weekend, or this film is most likely to provide a desired experience. He or she then participates in the hope that the experience will result.

Institutions which are meaning makers, then, rely on experiences to communicate their meanings. For no one changes his or her beliefs or values, even about trivial matters, unless something has happened to make a new or transformed value necessary. Those concerned to communicate a meaning must also provide an experience that connects the message with the personal interests of the hearer. This insight is not a new one. Good teachers, for example, have always done much more than expound general ideas. They have linked ideas to dramatic narrative, presented them in ways designed to intrigue the hearers, and have themselves furnished role models for students. The result is an experience, not just a lecture. In the same way, religious worship is often a dramatic composite of music, spoken word, movement, color, and even smell, all working together to communicate the myth. What is relatively new among meaning-making institutions is not reliance on experience, but a rapidly developing *technology* of experience. Sophisticated multi-dimensional environments are being constructed which make the traditional Sunday morning service seem anachronistic. And we can expect that meaning-making institutions will continue to refine their methods.

Values

We decided that the best way to understand the experiences being offered by religious groups was to ask the groups and their members about their values. In other words, values were used in the study as indicators of the ways religious communities were providing experience and meaning to their members.

For the purposes of this study, we defined values as Milton Rokeach does: "the affective priorities that guide one's life in the world."[20] Rokeach refers to values as basic beliefs about life and divides them into a central region, an intermediate region, and a peripheral region. In the central region are "primitive" beliefs, so called because they are often formed early in life without critical reflection and with the assumption that everyone else shares them. The content of the beliefs includes the nature of the physical world, the self, and the generalized other. In the intermediate region are beliefs in and about the nature of authority—beliefs about the people and institutions that help us form a picture of the world we live in. In the peripheral region are "attitudes," i.e., beliefs derived from authority and applied to specific situations. Judaeo-Christian values are in Rokeach's central and intermediate regions, because they are meant to order life, to distinguish what is more important and what is less important, and, therefore, to furnish a framework for all of life, within which one may set priorities in relation to daily living and life crises.

The attitudes lie in what Rokeach calls the peripheral region. An attitude is "an enduring organization of several beliefs focused on a specific object . . . or situation, predisposing one to respond in some peripheral manner."[21] Values are distinguished from attitudes because they transcend specific objects and situations; they have to do with modes of conduct and end-states of existence. "To say that a person 'has a value' is to say that he has an enduring belief that a particular mode of conduct or that a particular end-state of existence is personally and socially preferable to alternative modes of conduct or end-states of existence. . . . So defined, a value is a standard or criterion that serves a number of important purposes in our daily lives; it is a standard that tells us how to act or what to want; it is a standard that tells us what attitudes we should hold; it is a standard we employ to justify, to morally judge, and to compare ourselves with others."[22]

There are two ways to study values. The first is to examine them in terms of their content, as Rokeach does. The second is to examine the *process* that results in values, or the process of valuing. We may define the valuing process as the way in which a person evolves general guides to behavior out of his or her experience and applies them to decision making and action. Raths, Harmin, and Simon point out that "the conditions under which behavior is guided, in which values work, typically involve conflicting demands, a weighing and a balancing, and finally an action that reflects a multitude of forces. Thus, values seldom function in a pure and abstract form. Complicated judgments are involved and what is really valued is reflected in the outcome of life as it is finally lived."[23] The authors suggest that the valuing process has three aspects: choosing, prizing, and acting. Choosing implies that alternative courses of action can be conceived, and that the person is free to select from among the alternatives. Prizing is taking responsibility for, or "owning" and affirming the decision one is making, and communicating it publicly. Acting is the implementation of the decision in some stable pattern of consistent behavior. "These three processes collectively define valuing. Results of the valuing process are called values."[24]

We can locate and study the values and valuing processes of religious groups in at least two ways. First, they are formally articulated in the theologies, charters, and goals of groups, and in the characteristic language the group uses to describe its activities and life. Values, as formally articulated, however, do not always bear a close relationship to actual operating principles. So, although it is important to chart formal values, it is also important to describe the actual valuing processes that people use. Because most guides to decision making, such as "common sense," are habitual and traditional, they do not need to be consciously articulated. In fact, a person cannot clearly tell before acting on a matter what his or her values are, and how they are used in the valuing process. This is not because he or she just "hasn't thought about it." Values are essentially vague because they are modified or elaborated, if not actually created, in the continuing process of sensible decision making and action.[25]

In a time of social and cultural change, traditional assumptions about how to act in the social world do not work so well. To paraphrase Alfred Schutz: what I assume, what I assume you assume as well, and what I assume that you assume the same for me, can no longer be so safely assumed.[26] Precisely because the social world and the way I operate in it can no longer be taken for granted, and because I am asked to make increasing numbers of personal choices instead of relying on traditional structures, my valuing becomes problematic. It does not work in the taken-for-granted way it used to, and I must subject my valuing to critical examination. This study focused especially on those areas where groups were finding the traditional myths, values, and organizational forms inadequate, and were, therefore, experimenting with new beliefs or methods.

Where to Look for Experience

Where does one look for religious groups offering meaning-laden experiences to persons coping with the opportunities and burdens of being an individual in a pluralistic and changing society?

We began by considering the growth trends among religious bodies noted in the first chapter. The Pentecostal movement is perhaps the fastest growing phenomenon in American religious life. Clearly, examples of Pentecostal groups should be included in the study. Other smaller movements that can be identified are the increased interest in Hebrew studies among Jewish college students; the movement of "house churches," which depend on the methods and lifestyles of the human potential movement; and the spontaneous formation of gospel choruses by black college students in revolt against the white music of the official chapel choirs.

But it is also possible to speculate about trends that might logically emerge, given what we know about the changing attitudes and behavior of people now in organized religious groups. For example, in his book, *A Study of Generations,* Merton Strommen reports on the characteristics of Lutheran young people.[27] Based on Strommen's observations, we can anticipate and seek out groups that are forming with those dominant characteristics.

Moving from relatively "hard" data like the Strommen study to some "softer" hunches, we decided to look carefully at some of the secular forecasts of social and cultural changes to which people will have to respond in the future. If these forcasts are accurate, the groups which are addressing the problems raised by the projected changes will probably have a corner on the future of religion. So we explored this path.

We found indications that the expansion of science and

technology and the consequent increase of novelty as a
way of life will interact with population growth to produce
large, complex, and ever-changing organizations. As a
result, America faces increasing diversity of values; temporary and changing careers, communities, and lifestyles;
and a vast proliferation of choices. Logically, then, we
should look for groups addressing the problem of "over-
choice" by helping people to learn, love, and choose in an
increasingly complex environment. The difficulty with
this approach, of course, is that it depends on the myths
and assumptions of the secular forecasters, who may have
no better clues to the future than the traditional religious
groups themselves.

The problem we faced in the Insearch study in selecting
religious groups to examine is similar to the problem that
confronted Abraham Maslow in his famous study of "self-
actualizing" people. Maslow was interested not in the
question, "What are human beings like on the average?"
but, "Of what are human beings capable?"[28] In the same
way we were interested not in the question, "What is the
average state of religion in the culture?" but, "What is
possible for religious communities in this culture in providing meaning-laden experiences?" The further assumption is that such groups will give important clues about the
changing shape of religion in this culture. Presumably, we
can learn from lively groups what religious communities
can, and perhaps will, become.

In selecting "superior" human beings, Maslow at least
had certain guidelines provided by psychiatric interviews,
projective tests, performance tests, and other instruments
of the art of psychological assessment.[29] But selecting the
most "faithful" or "promising" or "vital" religious communities involves one in a host of theological judgments
on which there is no consensus (otherwise the New Israel
and the one universal church would have appeared in
manifest visible form long ago). Nevertheless, we are not

entirely without resources. Maslow states that "the health-
iest people (or the most creative, or the strongest, or the
wisest, or the saintliest) can be used . . . as advanced
scouts, or more sensitive perceivers, to tell us less sensitive
ones what it is we value."[30] Therefore, although it is a
fruitless task to try to establish an operational definition
of a "superior religious community in the Judaeo-Christian tradition," it is a quite feasible task to identify a fairly
large number of persons who represent the spectrum of
that tradition, and whose range of experience and insight-
fulness suggest that their nominations of vital religious
communities can be taken seriously. Then one can study
a representative number of the groups they suggest. And
this is essentially how we proceeded. We asked colleagues
whose faith and judgment we trusted, and their colleagues, and eventually a network of over 500 persons,
"Do you personally know any religious groups that are
quite vital and that may be saying something significant
about the future of religion in this culture?" Responses
came quickly, and we soon had well over 200 nominations
of great variety to choose from. The findings apply to the
groups studied and do not demonstrate or "prove" any-
thing about the general state of religion in America. They
do offer clues and hypotheses about trends, because the
descriptive and the normative meet at the edge of history.
Our respondents told us of groups in which they thought
what *should* be happening in religion in the future *was*
happening *now,* thus pointing the way to the hoped-for
future. When we looked at the great variety of groups, we
found certain dominant values, organizational forms, and
mission concerns. Together these values, forms, and concerns gave some picture of the realizable visions of religious groups and, also, of the changing shape of religion
in our culture, subject always to time and circumstance
and human decision.

3

Communities of Experience

SELECTING THE GROUPS

To find communities for study which held promise of significant religious life, we formed a panel of national and regional church and synagogue executives, scholars, ministers, lay leaders. We conferred also with researchers, trainers, and other specialists from a variety of theological traditions. These leaders were asked to nominate groups which they believed to be communities of outstanding religious vitality.

Clearly the groups in the Insearch Study do not constitute a statistically valid sample of American religious life. They simply represent a range of examples of what a number of unusually competent and well-informed leaders considered to be the most promising religious communities across the spectrum of the Judaeo-Christian tradition in 1972.

Over two hundred nominations were received. They seemed to fall into three major categories according to organizational form: *congregations, alternative communities,* and *special agencies.* Congregations we defined as "voluntary organizations, usually in a residential area, with a variety of mission activities, serving personal needs and social concerns and usually led by a paid staff." Urban and suburban congregations of all sizes were nominated. In addition, experimental congregations which had developed alternatives to typical congregational organization in staff leadership, member discipline, and community form were included. Alternative communities were defined as "groups who lived and/or worked together around certain commitments." In this category we included the only group in the study which is outside the Judaeo-Christian tradition, Tail of the Tiger, a Tibetan Buddhist meditative community. Specialized agencies in the study are "voluntary task forces or nonprofit corporations focusing on specific issues in education, community action, communication, or training resources."

Next, the groups could be categorized by theological tradition: Roman Catholic; conservative Protestant; liberal Protestant; Black Church; Orthodox, Conservative, and Reform Judaism; and groups which did not consider themselves either Christian or Jewish.

These two sets of categories formed a two-dimensional grid on which to place the nominations. We then selected one "outstanding example" in each cell of the grid for study. Selecting an "outstanding example" is clearly a subjective judgment, based on information received from the person who nominated the group and from other sources and documents from the group. The criteria by which we judged information about the groups are as follows: first, power and authenticity of community experience as reported by members and outsiders; second, effectiveness in changing lives of members and/or accomplishing mission tasks in the community as reported by members and outsiders; third, clarity and visibility of group identity and goals; fourth, when appropriate, the length of time the group has been able to sustain its vitality or existence; and last, when appropriate, growth in membership and budget.

The Insearch committee now had one religious community representative of each of the variations of organizational form and theological tradition. But there seemed to be other factors to be taken into account if we wanted to represent the range of nominations given to us. For example, the mission emphasis, or particular goals of the community. Urban and suburban congregations tend to have inclusive goals related to worship, evangelism, nurture of members, and services to the community; while experimental congregations, alternative communities, and specialized agencies often focus on a specific area, such as health care, child care, or political action. We wanted to represent the range of mission specializations.

Groups also varied according to racial and ethnic identity, age, sex, and socio-economic class. We wanted to represent those variations, too, in our study. Therefore, when the nominations in any one cell varied significantly, either in mission focus or social composition, we selected a third example to represent those differences.

Finally, although nominations came from all regions of the country, the groups studied happened to be mostly from the West and Northeast because of the availability of contacts and research teams there. Resources were insufficient to study all possible varieties of groups in each geographic region.

There was no way to develop a "representative sample" of groups in different categories. In some cases, the number of groups in a particular category is simply not known. In others, the category is so large, as for example in suburban congregations, that if it were represented in the study in proportion to its comparative strength, there would have been no resources to study the other categories.

Table I lists by organizational form and theological tradition the thirty-six groups that ultimately participated in the study. We tried unsuccessfully to include additional non-white and evangelical groups, and looked for examples of special categories like ecumenical clusters and Catholic and Black charismatic groups. Eighteen such groups were approached which did not, in the end, participate. These omissions are especially lamented in a study that purports to give glimpses of the future of religion in America. Hopefully, these areas of neglect will be remedied in future studies.

STUDYING THE GROUPS

The research design called for interviewing the leaders of each group, and choosing with the leaders a ten- to fifteen-member sample of the group that would include: leaders and members; persons central and peripheral to group life; short-term and long-term members; and representatives of the sub-group diversity (including racial and socio-economic) of the community. Participants in this sample were asked to fill out two questionnaires, which solicited such information as age, sex, occupation, living situations, religious affiliation, political beliefs and activities, and participation in other voluntary organizations. The questionnaires included questions about life beliefs and values; religious experiences, beliefs, and knowledge; psychological preferences; and a range of questions about participation in the religious groups being studied.

In addition to filling out the questionnaires, the sample members attended a three- to six-hour group interview with a two-person research team. One person on the team was an experienced researcher and trainer, usually known to the community before the project. The other person videotaped this interview for later analysis by a coding team. The group interview was designed to elicit the group's history; characteristics of its internal life such as climate, communication, decision-making processes, and special language; its goals, strategies, and typical activi-

TABLE I

Groups Participating in the Study

(For a fuller description see Appendix A, page 141)

	CONGREGATIONS	ALTERNATE COMMUNITIES	SPECIAL AGENCIES
Roman Catholic	St. Francis de Sales Cathedral Study and Discussion Group	St. John's Abbey Abbey of New Clairvaux St. Justin's Convent	Emmaus House
Conservative Protestant	King's Temple Prince of Peace American Lutheran Church	Lighthouse Ranch Teen Challenge	Project Challenge Vanguard Magazine
Liberal Protestant	Church of the Celebration COACT Now Church St. Francis Presbyterian Church Glide Memorial United Methodist Church	Open End Rancho Colorado	COMMIT Joint Health Venture For Love of Children Task Force
(Transitional Church)			
Black Church	Koinonia Missionary Baptist Church		Chicago Center for Black Religious Studies
Jewish	Congregation Solel Lincoln Square Synagogue	Brandeis Camp Institute Havurat Shalom	Jewish Parents Institute Sh'ma
Not Explicitly Related to Judaeo-Christian Tradition	Religious Science and Unity Congregation	Onager Family Spirit of '76 Tail of the Tiger	New Community Projects Earthlight

ties; and whatever else the group wished to share with the interviewers. Some of the data gathered are reported later in this volume. Brief case studies were also prepared (see Appendix A), as well as videotape presentations.

THE GROUPS CLUSTER AROUND SIX MAJOR CONCERNS

We know now how the groups were selected and studied in the Insearch project. It is time to begin examining the fruits of that project, to discuss the groups themselves.

We have noted that the groups represent virtually every part of the Judaeo-Christian tradition. But are there some common themes that cut across the diversity of the groups in the study? There do seem, in fact, to be a small number of major concerns that characterize and influence both the myth and the community form of our groups, whether Catholic, Protestant, Jewish, or non-Judaeo-Christian. The method we used to uncover these common themes was to sort out which groups were most like which other groups in the study in terms of their purposes, goals, and major activities. Each group's record of goals, meaningful experiences, and current activities was subjected to a statistical treatment called "cluster analysis," which pairs the groups that are most similar to each other, and then increases the size of the clusters, one by one, until all the groups are clustered together.[1] The first pair represents the two groups closest to each other of all the groups in the study in terms of goals, activities, and common life. The next pair represents the second closest groups and so on through decreasing levels of similarity until all the groups are clustered.

The clusters containing four to six groups seemed to represent six distinctive emphases or specializations of the religious groups in the study, which transect the categories of theological tradition and organizational form by which the communities were originally chosen. This analysis should be seen as one method of identifying patterns of commonality or major themes by which these religious groups are addressing the problems of contemporary culture. Following are the clusters, an interpretation of each, the groups that comprise it, and a case study illustrating each cluster.

The New Creation

The groups in the first cluster have in common a serious interest in relating their theological traditions to the pressing problems of the social order. This might be called "the liberal vocation"—a sustained encounter between the heritage of faith and society in which both are transformed. New occasions teach new duties. It is not sufficient simply to repeat the verities of faith; they must be rethought, reformulated, rediscovered in the process of co-struggling with God to bring about the new creation promised by faith. But the basis of social concern is not simply pragmatic or humanitarian; it is consciously, intentionally, and as comprehensively as possible grounded in faith. The groups of the new creation cluster hold together two commitments—to the continuing theological enterprise, and to the transformation of the world according to the insights of faith. Four groups are represented in the first pairings in this cluster: Emmaus House, Koinonia Missionary Baptist Church, Chicago Center for Black Religious Studies, and *Sh'ma*. Emmaus is grounded in the Catholic Worker Movement and has been a center for Catholic action for two decades. Koinonia and the Chicago Center represent the theological vitality and empowerment struggles of the Black church, and *Sh'ma* is an expression of the intense sensitivity to social reality of

Judaism. In a later cluster, these four groups are joined by the Catholic Study and Discussion Group, Havurat Shalom, and Now Church, which express the same concerns for fresh theological approach to all of life. As an example, not necessarily typical, of "New Creation" groups, *Sh'ma* is especially interesting.

Sh'ma

For a number of years, Eugene Borowitz had been thinking and talking to his friends about beginning a journal which would relate Jewish values and tradition to social concerns. In December, 1969, Borowitz, along with Stephen Schwarzchild, Arnold Wolf, and others decided that the time had come to launch such a venture; there was great interest in the Jewish community about social issues, and Borowitz, from New York, now had time to serve as volunteer editor. The model for the kind of magazine the group wanted was *Christianity and Crisis,* though they all recognized that no Jewish Reinhold Niebuhr was available and that this magazine would have to be pluralistic in its social attitudes.

In February, 1970, the first meeting was held with some contributing editors, and the decision was made to produce two trial issues in May and June of that year. The response to the trial balloons considerably exceeded the editors' expectations, and the regular bi-weekly journal was instituted as of November, 1970. Individual and bulk subscriptions came pouring in, unsolicited articles began to arrive, and the magazine improved in quality and became established in the Jewish community. It also received fairly wide publicity. Articles about *Sh'ma* appeared in *Time* magazine and the Sunday *New York Times* Op-Ed page. The assistant editor was both amused and pleased when *Sh'ma* appeared as the answer to a question in the religious category on "Jeopardy," a popular daytime television quiz program. *Sh'ma*'s continuing acceptance in the Jewish community was also marked by the willingness of Rabbi David Bleich, Orthodox expert on Jewish law, to serve as a contributing editor.

Eugene Borowitz, who is a professor of Jewish thought at Hebrew Union College, City College, and Princeton University, serves the journal as a volunteer, as do the members of the Jewish intellectual community who function as contributing editors. The assistant editor is the only salaried person. Because *Sh'ma* is so entirely the creation of Gene Borowitz, our understanding of its basic purpose is derived from his own articulation of his vision, rather than from a group interview. The ostensible purpose of the magazine is to relate Jewish thought to social concerns through a journal of opinion and dialectic. The journal's market consists of those Jewish intellectuals who still identify themselves actively with the Jewish religious community. A latent but equally significant purpose is to address the loneliness and sense of being out of place which is a major affliction of thoughtful Jews.

Sh'ma is more than something to read; it offers its 6500 subscribers a way to enter into dialogue with each other. Borowitz wants to teach Jews how to argue with each other again, how to differ, how to disagree, how to enter into sharp but appropriate Jewish dialectic. His vision is "to build a community," not around social activism as such, nor around a new institution or program, but relying solely upon the advancement and discussions of ideas. On reading this description, Borowitz commented: "Please keep in mind that I have a sense of humor as well as of reality. While I would like to see a community sense develop around *Sh'ma,* I recognize how evanescent bi-weekly contact with a journal, forty weeks a year is. I am happy that we/I am producing a good magazine. I hope we can do more with it—but I know how faint that sort of hope is."

Evidently *Sh'ma* has had some success in implementing this vision. It confronts issues facing Jews directly and presents them concisely so that eight pages give the reader more to think about than other journals several times its length. It intends to apply Jewish values to specific problems and to provide a platform for persons who do not have the opportunity to speak through established Jewish institutions. It is not a scholarly journal, but a journal of opinion, and represents the diversity of views and issues within the Jewish community. *Sh'ma* does not take editorial stands or present a monolithic viewpoint, but provides a way to hammer out issues from many different viewpoints.

Sh'ma may be trend-setting in its choice of communications as a method for building community. It reflects a wide interest among religious groups in presenting theological, political, or cultural concerns through the communications media. *Sh'ma* is interesting as well because it travels light. With a minimal paid staff, as Borowitz points out, as long as *Sh'ma* is alive and bright and breaking new ground, it will continue; but when its time is past, it can simply close up shop. The editor's aim, in his words, is "community without organization." He concludes, "This is one experiment in creating a sense of togetherness without meetings, buildings, or commitment to common action other than discussion despite difference. I am pleased that we continue to reach out to new people to join the discussion. By contributing, with or without invitation, such new people continue to participate."

The Heritage of Faith

An Orthodox synagogue (Lincoln Square), a Benedictine monastery (St. John's Abbey), an urban Roman Catholic cathedral (St. Francis de Sales), and an American Lutheran suburban parish (Prince of Peace), compose this cluster of groups, which together affirm an orthodoxy of belief, and through that orthodoxy, a vital contemporary religious life. The local congregations in this cluster report rapid growth in membership and attendance. Despite the general erosion of belief in the culture, or perhaps because of it, a clear, thoughtfully presented orthodox theology has a powerful appeal in the midst of contemporary cultural fragmentation. St. Francis de Sales presents an interesting example of the appeal of traditional beliefs and organizational forms, presented in a fresh and imaginative way.

St. Francis de Sales Cathedral

The Roman Catholic cathedral, in Oakland, California, sits in the heart of the city surrounded on one side by the ghetto which gave birth to the Black Panther Party, and on the other by downtown commercial buildings and middle- to high-income residence hotels. The Greyhound bus depot, located across the street, is flanked by numerous bars and cheap rooming houses, inhabited by transients, wayfarers, and assorted misfits along with a large population of elderly people, too poor to afford better accommodations. Prostitution, drugs, and crime are heavy in this area. The other half of the parish—at the edge of the groomed Lake Merritt Park—houses the retired and well-pensioned middle class along with wealthy business establishments.

For twenty-six years, St. Francis de Sales church and school complex was managed by an aging pastor whose response to the radical change in the area was almost complete insulation. When Oakland became an independent diocese and St. Francis de Sales was designated its cathedral, a new pastor was appointed.

In September, 1968, the young new pastor decided to try a new approach in ministering to the needs of the parish. His first step was to share all policymaking and parish responsibilities with a team consisting of his two associate pastors and the four nuns who taught in the school. After evaluating priorities, the team decided to tackle what they considered the two most important, and put available money and effort into the Sunday worship services and the parish school.

Father Donald Osuna, one of the two associate pastors and a specialist in the liturgy, coordinated the liturgical revitalization of St. Francis de Sales. With the help of the lay choir director, he developed a contemporary service called "Creative Celebration." A choir of thirty voices and an instrumental ensemble of professional musicians, along with the singing congregation provide music in every idiom from Bach to rock. Visual presentations (films, slides, and banners) and theater pieces (skits and dramatic readings) help to put the Gospel message across with added emphasis. The preaching is designed to be "more a testimony than a sermon, a demonstration and celebration of Christian oneness." Consistent efforts are made to teach people to participate actively in the liturgy, and to "get over their inhibitions." Each celebration is well planned and tied

together so that the verbal, musical, and visual elements reinforce the central theme of the worship service. Four times a year
a special series is offered in which a given topic such as "Humor" or "Play" or "Faces in the Revolution" is treated with
ingenuity and originality.

As a result of sustained and very creative attention to liturgy,
attendance went from 500 to overflow crowds of up to 1100 at
the 10:30 A.M. mass within two years. One must now get to mass
before 10:00 A.M. in order to obtain a seat, and during the
service, people are "standing in the aisles, sitting in the chancel
and in front of the church on the floor."

The parochial school, the second priority, included 70%
black, 20% Latin, and 10% white, non-Latin students. Parents,
at first quite passive in their relationship to the school, were
gradually persuaded to become more active. Through a series of
wine tasting parties beginning in the fall of 1970, the parents'
club raised funds for some needed remodeling. In the same fall,
non-graded programs were started in the sixth through eighth
grades, and the school is currently experimenting with open
classrooms and a variety of curricula related to interpersonal
experience. The school attempts to expose the students, who
come from mostly ghetto homes, to a wide variety of experiences
through field trips outside the city, as well as a sense of "family"
and mutual friendship with the faculty.

In the fall of 1969, Sister Thomasine McMahon, an experienced worker among the elderly, joined the parish staff.
Under her direction, a third priority was adopted—programs
for the aged. She began such activities as Thanksgiving and
Christmas dinners for those without families, person-to-person
visits with shut-ins and those in convalescent hospitals, liaisons
between church and civic programs for the aged.

The priests and nuns constitute the management team of the
parish, which meets weekly, and evidently has good working
relationships and open communication. The team seems to work
with considerable skill and sophistication. The leaders set the
priorities, then call in professional consulting agencies to gather
data about the needs in the community and suggest strategies.
The leaders then decide on goals and call on persons and groups
in the parish to implement their plans. Although informal feed-

back from lay people comes from the choir on the liturgy, the parents' club in the school, and the varied face-to-face relationships of Sister Thomasine with the aged, one professional remarked in the group interview that this was "the first time we have heard what lay people think." In the interview, interest was expressed in a lay parish council to share in the administration of the church, but the idea was not encouraged.

The parish has about 3000 members, of whom about 2000 participate in some parish organization. An estimated 40% are male, and ages range from infants to the aged. Sixty percent are white, 30% black, 10% Latin and others. Although the congregation is mostly lower- and middle-class, the parish boundaries reach from the ghetto to the upper-class residential area above Oakland, so, according to the researcher, "on any given Sunday, the very poor and the very rich are side by side in this cathedral."

The traditional as well as the novel may be trend-setting for the future of religion. St. Francis de Sales is an example of a church doing very well what a post-Vatican II urban Catholic parish can do, in vitality of liturgy, compassion and effectiveness of social service in the area, and creative teaching in the parochial school. The decision making is also traditional, with relatively little lay participation. The church carries out traditional ministries, yet avails itself of the best sophisticated contemporary resources in doing so. And it seems to be quite successful, measured by the indicators of morale, sense of community, excitement, and growth. There seems to still be a place for the residential congregation carrying out traditional ministries well, and avoiding stereotyped or mediocre methods.

During the interview, the group articulated the purpose of the church: "To promote the experience of Christian joy and active Christian concern for others. The stated goals of the group paralleled the descriptions of the church's three priorities (liturgy, the school, and the aged): "to show our people that we care, we value them as people"; to relate to other agencies in the community; and to have fun and avoid complacency. Characteristically, the language reflects these goals, employing liturgical phrases such as "God loves you." The aims of the church seem to be consistent with its actual activities and programs. There is a quality of friendship, openness, and community in the group of people that comprise the parish of St. Francis de Sales.

To Walk in His Ways

There is an identifiable cluster of groups which emphasize the living of one's own personal life according to the imperatives of faith. The concern of these groups is for personal morality, interpersonal ethics, and a lifestyle embraced by tradition. In an unpublished paper on our findings, Martin Marty remarked that "the ritual-liturgical-*devotional*-meditative syndrome has returned. . . . More attention is being paid to almost trivial behavioral detail. By this I do not mean ethics and moral injunctions so much as quasi-ceremonial routines and lifestyles."[1] It would be tempting to call these people "holiness groups" except for the fact that the first cluster of four includes the Jewish Parents' Institute, representing secular Judaism. However, this group shares with the others a concern for developing personal living styles out of tradition. Two groups, Teen Challenge and Project Challenge, are conservative Protestant organizations, and the last group is a Trappist monastery, New Clairvaux. In a later pairing, they are joined by four more communities with the same concern for personal living according to faith: Congregation Solel, Brandeis Camp, King's Temple, and Lighthouse Ranch. A representative example of these groups is New Clairvaux monastery.

The Abbey of New Clairvaux

New Clairvaux, a Trappist monastery in Vina, California, was begun in 1955 when the order decided to found a house on the West Coast. The monastery supports itself on the income of a 586-acre farm which grows prunes and English walnuts in northern California's Sacramento Valley. In earlier days the brothers and fathers did all the work themselves. Now, with fewer members in the community, some outside labor is needed.

One father told me that Trappists were formerly referred to as "the Marine Corps of the Catholic Church." "As long as Trappists stand firm, the Church will stand firm." Following the rule of St. Benedict in one of its most rigorous forms, the order followed the strict discipline of silence and accompanying austerities, with a sense of representing the best of Catholic asceticism, until Vatican II. In the mid-sixties, the house at Vina was shaken by the winds of change from Rome. In 1965, the community began a series of discussions on how to implement *aggiornamento*. As one father summarized it, "We had to learn how to interact with each other." Detailed instructions for the living of each part of the day now had to make room for personal interaction, and, as one said, "for the recognition that now each person was responsible for his own spiritual growth and could no longer simply depend on the rules of the community."

Such change did not take place without tension and conflict. In 1968, the first abbot resigned and was succeeded by a person much less directive in style. The present superior seems to strike a balance between the authoritativeness of the first and the more open style of the second abbot. In 1970 a fire destroyed the monastery buildings. After the initial shock ("How could God let this happen to us?"), the community began rebuilding with a firmer intention to shape their environment to nurture their common life.

In spite of the changes, New Clairvaux remains cloistered. Members do not leave the abbey except for special purposes. The monks arise every morning at 3:15 and combine meditation, hard work on the farm, and study throughout the day within a liturgical framework in the Benedictine fashion. "Trailer Day," the one day a month that each monk spends in a house trailer on the grounds, exempt from community horarium, is a cherished privilege.

In recent years both Zen Buddhism and Pentecostal experience have been appropriated by monks within the Cistercian framework. Zen is currently little-used, but regular Pentecostal meetings attended by several monks from the community are held on the grounds. Those monks who have received the Baptism of the Holy Ghost—speaking in tongues—believe it can be traced to the early experiences of eremites in the Egyptian desert in the early centuries of Christianity.

The community began with 28 members in 1955, grew to about 50 in the intervening years, and has now decreased to 25 resident monks, of whom seven are priests. Ages range from 24 to 70 with the average age in the forties. There is one native Mexican in the community; the rest are white Americans.

The superior is very much a father to the community. He does not believe in total democracy for monks, but is moving toward a "systemic" form of government, in which committees make recommendations on a variety of matters, but the final decision is reserved to himself or to a community vote.

During the group interview, the monks said their purpose was to be a community totally oriented toward the experience of the living God. The aims of union with God and community with one another are fulfilled through the structures of monastic life —"Life under the rule and under the abbot." There is little that is idiosyncratic in expression in the discussion of group goals and purpose—the monks have learned to speak a common language as they have learned to live a common discipline. "Trailer Day," the one day a month of leisure from the discipline, is especially valued as is the "Palace of Culture," a delightful bit of irony referring to the back room in the tractor shed where a phonograph and some records and books are available.

One fails to communicate what New Clairvaux is about unless one describes being with these quiet, serene men, working at simple manual tasks under the dry sun, amid the gentle wind and the walnut trees. At evening and in the darkness before morning, they are quietly transformed by their robes. In the liturgy, they sing modestly but with considerable sophistication, and the farmhand who is now priest offers the Eucharist with dignity and power. But above all, the category of change seems irrelevant here. It is present, of course, in the building of new cells, and in the struggle to partially replace individual obedience with community responsibility. The Mass and the rule, however, remain. And one either accepts the premise, or one does not. "Going toward God" is either life's magnificent end and daily activity, or it is not. Praying for the salvation of the world is either efficacious in the divine economy, or it is not. The sense of "givenness" overwhelms—the Mass is given; the chant is given; the sun and the world are given; God is given. And that may even be trend-setting—the clear alternative to majority values of change, or progress; or corporate struggle for power, or personal differentiation. It is not trend-setting if one judges by the declining number of monks, but then by what criteria does one decide?

At Work in the World

A cluster of five groups represents a more humanitarian or pragmatic commitment to social action than the new creation groups described earlier. While they join the new creation groups in one of the final clusters in the analysis, they are distinguished from them by a less theological and more pragmatic approach to social concerns. This does not necessarily imply less orthodoxy or even less theological interest; one of the groups is *Vanguard* magazine, based on a rigorous neo-Calvinism. But the aim of group life is toward specific programs of social action rather than toward the generation of social concerns out of a comprehensive theological intention. In addition to *Vanguard,* the groups are: For Love of Children Task Force of the Church of Our Savior, St. Francis Presbyterian Church, Joint Health Venture, and COMMIT. COMMIT is described here because it also exemplifies the independent, specialized service agencies that are making an important contribution to contemporary church and synagogue life.

COMMIT

COMMIT is an independent non-profit corporation for training and consultation located in Los Angeles, working for social change through training and action programs in race relations, support of liberation and peace movements, and church organization development.

COMMIT works with a wide range of church and secular agencies. One large contract came from the U.S. Department of Health, Education and Welfare for a job training project in Dallas. Perhaps the largest program has been "Project Understanding," which organized clusters of white, suburban churches for awareness and action training in the issues of racism. COMMIT helped organize clergy and laity throughout southern California to support several antiwar projects. Another large effort developed a network of resources for continuing education for clergy in southern California. In addition to specific contracts for training and consulting, COMMIT holds a number of courses each spring and fall, and supervises seminary students in field work.

As the program of COMMIT has grown, so has the staff. In 1967 there were two staff; currently there are six trainers on the staff. One trainer was originally a secretary on the staff who grew professionally until she was working fulltime as a trainer, specializing in women's issues, such as finding ways for women to break out of dead-end jobs. There are now two women, one black and the other Chicano, on the training staff.

The staff of COMMIT operates in a collegial style, in which, according to the researcher, the director gives space and freedom to the staff, but still holds them accountable for goals set by the staff and board. Staff are expected to be self-starters. Each one is encouraged to develop and implement his or her own contracts. The staff meets for a half-day every two weeks; the board, which includes 53 members, primarily local judicatory officials, meets quarterly.

Speed Leas, the director, described his role as "being responsible for this organization," and counted this responsibility the most meaningful part of his work. He is clearly director of the organization and he makes all personnel decisions. COMMIT's director is an example of the entrepreneur in developing religious groups. He is not a prophetic preacher or inspired teacher, but he is skilled in organizing, hustling, and managing. In his own professional life and in the organization that he directs, Speed models the skills he offers to teach others. The researcher comments, "One has the sense of a well-run organization with staff and board feeling a deep commitment to goals, and a sense of confidence. There is honesty among all about failures as well as an over-all sense of being part of an effective, skillful organization. This charisma is much needed by churches and synagogues, and its presence is a hopeful sign for the future of organized religion."

COMMIT is an example of the increasing number of independent agencies offering specialized resources to local congregations and to clergy. In the 1960s, a number of such agencies developed and flourished as it became clear that religious organizations and their leadership needed specialized training and resources in order to relate to the needs of a changing society. There are now well over one hundred of what might be generally termed "continuing education agencies" across the country, some affiliated with larger institutions such as seminaries, some independent. Some of these new agencies offer specialized services, such as career counseling for clergy or action training. Because of the need for these resources, such agencies will probably continue to exist and even expand, despite the increasing difficulties in funding.

COMMIT is also interesting because of the nature of the training it provides: "exposure, action, and reflection." Unlike most other types of training or continuing education, groups, COMMIT first exposes people to the needs of oppressed groups in society. Sometimes people are not aware of their own alienation and oppression. Sometimes they are not aware of or do not understand the needs of other oppressed groups. But in both cases COMMIT insists that the oppression is caused by dysfunctional or exploitative institutional structures. COMMIT's training is designed to equip persons and groups with skills to change social structures to liberate and empower people.

COMMIT had to decide whether it would be solely a training agency for churches that want to become involved in social action, or whether it would also become directly involved in advocating and working for social change. This was a difficult and very important decision. If an agency trains others to work for social change but does not do so itself, it may become irrelevant and never develop the skills that groups need to be effective.

On the other hand, if it actively works for change, it may alienate its funding sources and provoke opposition from the community and the churches with which it wants to work. In June, 1971, COMMIT formally decided to be an agent for change itself. This decision was congruent with the vision of the director that the essential purpose of the group is "working for and with oppressed groups for their liberation."

The groups COMMIT wishes to work with include non-white communities, women, the poor, the elderly, and alienated and disenchanted middle-class persons in white suburban churches. COMMIT also wants to reach out to blue-collar workers who would usually support George Wallace. Organizing them on the basis of self-interest, as Saul Alinsky taught, COMMIT hopes to show these workers that at certain key points their self-interests align them with blacks, Chicanos, and other oppressed groups.

Personal Growth

Groups in the cluster are distinguished by their strong emphasis on the personal growth of their members. They tend to be single-minded in that aim, whether growth is understood in terms of interpersonal skills, meditation, or happiness, or is defined by each member for himself or herself. These groups represent an important new force on the religious scene, meeting the hunger for experience in a direct, personal way. They can be distinguished from the holiness groups by their lesser interest in relating personal growth to their religious heritage, and from the next cluster ("New Lifestyles") by their lesser interest in social critique. The groups in this personal growth cluster are: Church of the Celebration, New Thought Alliance, Tail of the Tiger, St. Justin's Convent, and Open End. Open End is a particularly interesting example of a group which uses methods drawn from the human potential movement to meet members' needs for personal growth and supportive community.

Open End

Open End is a non-residential community in San Rafael, California, that seeks to offer "alternative" and deeper levels of community to middle-class suburbanites. It emphasizes both the human potential and sensitivity training approaches. Started by Barbara and Frank Potter in Marin County in 1965, Open End now has a membership of more than 250, and activities ranging from encounter groups, dance therapy, and personal counseling to ski and hiking weekends. The community publishes a monthly newsletter, provides consultant services for groups attempting to form new communities, and serves as the communication center for Well Being, a national association of new or "human" community-building groups.

A distinctive goal of Open End is to provide an ongoing environment or community in which members not only learn greater self-awareness and sensitivity to others, but also have an opportunity to live out their new sense of self with some of the same people who provided support and guidance during the initial change process. In fact, the existence of an ongoing community makes the change or humanization process a continuous one. A recent questionnaire sent out to members indicated that the most important goal for the majority was community— "warm and friendly relationships that offer the chance for deeper relationships instead of casual ones."

A second goal is to allow members a wide choice of community activity. This is provided by monthly activities that range from hiking to encounter groups. Giving and receiving support for personal involvement in social change is a third goal mentioned by some members.

Most of the approximately 250 members of Open End are middle-class and middle-aged, but there are some who are at opposite ends of the scale in both class and age. The ratio of women to men is 3 to 2. Frank Potter, the coordinator, sees himself as an enabler—not a guru—and attempts to balance policy setting between participation by the members and the final responsibility of the elected trustees.

Frank and Barbara Potter originally incorporated Open End as a non-profit organization with themselves and their lawyer as trustees. Today there are six additional trustees who are elected by the membership. Trustees and members attend group meetings called Open Forum at which the present and future directions of Open End are discussed. After these meetings, the nine trustees take final responsibility for establishing policy.

Members pay $12 monthly dues (tax deductible) which allows them to participate in as many activities as they wish. There is a special rate of $2 per month for students. Scholarships are available for those who cannot afford membership dues. These funds provide a salary for the full-time coordinator Frank Potter, and pay the operating costs of Open End, including the rental of a large house and several other buildings where the day-to-day operations and some of the group meetings are held.

Early in the life of Open End, the coordinator and non-member professionals were used extensively as group leaders. Now many groups meet in the homes of members who are also group leaders. These group leaders meet monthly for training.

Open End is also an interesting example of the intentional use of the insights and methods of the human potential movement to address traditionally religious issues of community, self-identity, vocation, and the shaping of values. While Open End itself has no creed, it addresses religious needs in ways that are in historical continuity with the life of the Church. Falling on the religious continuum between Judaeo-Christian groups and humanistic groups which take their values from some aspect of their culture, Open End illustrates the contest of myths, the loss of traditional theological language, and the searching for new language which makes sense in the light of the value issues of contemporary life. Groups like Open End seem to be searching for the kind of mythic forms which express members' religious convictions and their experiences, both individual and shared.

Finally, Open End illustrates an alternative financial base for a local congregation. The monthly dues offer enough capital to support the minimal paid leadership, whose primary responsibility is generating new program ideas and encouraging members to organize labs or form groups that appeal to them. Thus, the financial support of the members is directly tied to their participation and experiences, and a large and vital program can be sustained.

New Lifestyles

The final cluster of groups seeks to live a new lifestyle usually modeled on that coalition of the young, the black, and the dissatisfied middle-aged called the counterculture. Personal growth is a main objective of these groups, sought in the form of alternatives to prevailing societal values and organizational structures. Group goals include changing social structures or developing viable counter-communities and institutions in order to foster personal growth. The lifestyle groups include: New Community Projects, COACT, Glide Memorial Church, the Onager Family, Earthlight, Spirit of '76, and Rancho Colorado. Glide Church is interesting for many reasons, perhaps the most important being that it represents what has been called a "transitional church." Transitional churches exist in changing racial and ethnic neighborhoods, where they attempt to develop effective ministries to their shifting constituencies.

Glide Memorial Church

Glide Memorial Church is set "in the heart of the tenderloin area of San Francisco. The San Francisco Hilton is across the street on one corner. On other corners are pornographic bookstores, pornographic movies, prostitutes, both male and female, and pimps. Lots of winos are either sitting or staggering along the street at night." Through the years the church has become known throughout the country for its innovative and even controversial programs of service to the neglected—ethnic and racial groups, the poor, women, homosexuals, and the elderly.

In 1967, Cecil Williams, a black clergyman, was chosen to be the new pastor. At this time, when the flower children were flourishing in San Francisco, the church held an "invisible circus" for them, which is remembered as the "first pound at the door by the community," and which was the beginning of a more intentional relationship between the church and the surrounding neighborhood.

Pastor Williams also paid particular attention to the worship life of the church. Glide members were the only group interviewed who mentioned Christmas and Easter festivals as high points in the life of the church. Under Williams's influence, the traditional worship service became contemporary and informal. The choir was dropped, a full-time rock band arrived, light shows were presented in the service, the preacher stopped wearing his robe and grew a beard, the organ was taken out and the gold cross on the altar came down. As one member said, "Everything came down, or rather, everything went up." The researcher commented that in the service "a real celebrative feeling is created in which persons of all ages participate rather boisterously and actively."

By the fall of 1971, according to the group interview, people were "coming through the ceiling." A number of community action programs had been initiated, not without active resistance on the part of the community. In April, 1972, a shot was fired through the pastor's window. Once the Sunday service was held outside on the street because of a bomb scare.

The group identified its basic purpose as "freedom from bondage." Freedom includes the liberation of white middle-class people from the bondage of separation from the rest of the human family as well as the freedom of oppressed minorities. The theme that ran through the entire interview was bringing together people with different human needs, from different races, different cultures, different social and economic situations, to love and understand each other and to work together for liberation. The group emphasized affirming and accepting different lifestyles.

Action programs include participation in political campaigns, and a variety of programs on drug abuse and sex education run by Glide Urban Center. The group is against drug use and wants to communicate the possibility of being high, of living a satisfying and joyous life, without drugs. The sex education program is a courageous and open exploration of human sexuality, with a concern to help people see sexuality as a means of liberation.

The church is one of three interrelated organizations including Glide Foundation, the funding organization, and Glide Urban Center, which mounts many of the more specialized ministries. The staff of the church, in cooperation with the Foundation and the Urban Center, sets policy, makes budgets, and runs programs. People participate in the programs according to their own interests. But equally important, members of the church bring programs or "people movements" into the church, which in turn provides staff, support, and facilities. This free-floating system of organization develops a diversity of programs that reflect members' personal interest and commitment. One woman, for example, recounted that after a Monday night family supper had been discontinued, she noticed that many of the street people had depended upon it for their own sustenance. She determined to keep the Monday night supper going on her own, and so she comes to the church once a week to organize and cook it, with the church continuing to provide financial support.

There is an interesting combination of unity and diversity in Glide. People either participate in ongoing programs, or develop new programs of their own. But all of this apparent diversity revolves around agreement on fundamental values based on the Gospel of Liberation preached by Reverend Williams and expressed in his black street language, which has become the language of the church. One member said, "We all have the same ultimate goal of freeing ourselves; there are simply different ways of bringing it about." In the individual questionnaires, people expressed very different ideas about God. But the varying theological viewpoints really intersect in the Gospel of Liberation. As one person said about American life: "A peaceful revolution is needed."

Glide Memorial Church is one of the most exciting examples in the country of a vital urban congregation serving the needs of all kinds of people in the center city. The church also offers an example of a creative use of endowment. At Glide, the endowment, rather than restricting the church's ability to take risks, has freed the church to move into controversial areas that could probably not be supported by most mainline Protestant churches in the inner city.

There is a third important reason for studying Glide Church. One of the most important trends in American religious life is the movement of nonwhites into the urban center, and, therefore, the existence of what James Hargett calls "transitional congregations," i.e., formerly white churches in the inner city which are increasingly surrounded by black and Spanish-speaking Americans. Hargett has suggested that how white Christianity deals with this challenge will largely determine its continuing viability in major metropolitan areas. Many of these churches move out to the suburbs along with the white parishioners. Another alternative is to develop programs in which the non-white presence is increasingly felt in the membership and in the power structure of the inner city church. Glide Church seems to be a rare and stunningly successful example of this strategy. Cecil Williams, by his charismatic preaching and leadership, has transformed Glide into a church whose basic culture in language, organization, and atmosphere has moved from white to more black than white—a church which is, therefore, able to attract and sustain the active involvement and leadership of both groups in the community.

These then are the religious communities from the various strands of the Judeao-Christian tradition that participated in the Insearch study. They do not constitute a representative sample of American Religious life. They were selected from nominations from a large panel of church and synagogue leaders as being on the growing tip of religious life in this culture. We have seen that there are a few themes that seem to characterize them, and that these themes cut across the theological and denominational lines. In order to find the implication of the study for the renewal of church and synagogue life, we need to look more closely at the members of these religious communities. What are their religious backgrounds and experiences? What motivates them to participate in these groups? And what can we say about the leaders of these communities?

4

Styles of Participation

The religious groups in our study can be looked at from the perspective of their central concerns as we did in chapter three. They can also be studied on the basis of the style of participation of their members. In the history of the study of religion, one of two styles of participation has been held to be of the essence. Whitehead believed religion was what man does with his solitude,[1] while Durkeim concluded that religion is society.[2] Throughout the study of religion there has been a continuing argument as to whether religion is essentially an individual matter, or a matter of participation in a community, or both, and if both, how they are balanced. In this study we actually uncovered three different ways by which persons express their faith: through activity in an organization, through close interpersonal relationships, and through personal religious experience and discipline. Let us look at each of these in turn.

ORGANIZATIONAL ACTIVITY

The first way by which people express their faith is organizational activity. The tradition teaches, and the individual who suscribes to this value believes, that attendance and activity in the organizational life of the church or synagogue is important in its own right. The emphasis may be on attending public worship, working on committees, or participating in corporate service activities. Each group has its own organizational activities in which members are required or encouraged to participate.

Participants in the study were asked a number of questions about their participation in their religious group. The responses were subjected to factor analysis. Factor analysis seeks out a small number of categories which underlie many different responses to a questionnaire. These few general categories may then sum up or explain the many different answers, and thus describe the values of participants in the study, as expressed on their questionnaires. (The numbers alongside each value or variable tell how close each variable is associated to the factor. The higher the number, the more closely it is associated with the factor and, therefore, the more important it is in determining the nature of the factor. A negative association means that the factor is partially defined by the very fact that it is so distant from the value.)

TABLE II

Organizational Activity

Number of Sabbaths attending worship	.75
Frequency of attending meetings	.72
Frequency of reading the Bible	.70
Self-rating of church or synagogue activity	.66
Frequency of prayer	.66
Percentage of income given in financial contribution	.65
Frequency of talking about religion with friends or co-workers	.52

These responses indicate that organizational activity is one of the important ways people participate in their religious groups. These individual questions which appeared in the organizational activity factor were answered significantly differently for the various religious groups—the number of Sabbaths attending worship, the self-rating of church or synagogue activity, and the frequency of attending meetings. Dividing the participants in the study into Roman Catholic, conservative Protestant, liberal Protestant, Jewish, and other religious groups, we found that certain types of organizational activities were more characteristic of certain traditions. As might be expected, Roman Catholics attended religious services more often. Jews rated themselves as most active in their groups, and liberal Protestants attended meetings most often. In response to the factor as a whole, Catholics participated most in organizational activity, followed by liberal Protestants, conservative Protestants, and Jews, with the "other" category last. These differences are significant statistically beyond the .001 level.

The organizational activity that lures members of these religious groups into participation is not a dull, inflexible routine. Even when the group is built around traditional beliefs and organizational forms, the vitality of the community comes from the fresh response and exciting representation of symbols and activities. We have seen earlier how St. Francis de Sales Cathedral in Oakland renewed its liturgy and organizational life. Churches and synagogues in contemporary culture are under increasing competition from other meaning-making institutions in society. If they expect their membership to be active, organizational activities must be meaningful and important.

An example of one of the groups in the study which is involved in a great deal of organizational activity, but in a fresh and non-bureaucratic way, is COACT.

COACT

COACT (Community of Active Christians Today) in Waco, Texas, adopted its corporate charter in the spring of 1970, after two years of developing a direction as a group and struggling to remain a part of the local First Lutheran Church. The group formed around members' desire to experiment with different Christian lifestyles and to make Christian living relevant for today—something they found increasingly difficult to do within the organized local churches of the community. The group entered into negotiations with synod officials and with another Lutheran church because of their concern for maintaining institutional ties and legitimizing their pastor's status. Several members left as a result of the group's final decision to become completely independent.

Ken Solberg, a Lutheran minister, became a part-time enabler for the community, and the group life consisted of weekly Sunday evening celebrations, weeknight small group discussions, and direct services and involvement with people-oriented programs in the Waco community.

The first characteristic of COACT which strikes the observer is the continuing involvement of members in a variety of human potential and human relations labs. One member said in the group interview, "That's what COACT is all about—labs and O.D. (organizational development)." A result of the lab experiences was the development of small groups with lay leadership for sharing, study, and support which formed and re-formed throughout the life of the larger group. One early lab experience became especially significant for the future mission and life of COACT. Five members attended a black-white confrontation and community awareness lab in September, 1970. Following this experience, they arranged for a similar lab in the community in November.

Out of those experiences, COACT decided to form a coalition with Project Self-Help, which aimed at generating jobs, free breakfasts, financial assistance, and community organization in the Black community. This program was evidently quite successful in catalyzing Black initiatives for Black empowerment. But an important side effect was to create an image in the community of COACT, and especially Ken Solberg, as "radicals." Because of the wide publicity the group was receiving, over 100 people from all over the state visited COACT on Memorial Day weekend the following spring, and initiated a network of mutual support which evidently still persists.

The group emphasizes, according to one of its brochures, that it is "people oriented—COACT is designed to stand or fall on the strength of its relationships." Fittingly, with this self-image, the next key event which stood out in members' memories was Labor Day weekend that year. COACT members planned a three-day party to celebrate their feelings of community. During the weekend, the baptism of a child adopted by one family was a high point of group identity.

In November of 1971, two key decisions were made which determined much of the organizational form of the group. Members decided that there was no further need for a part-time enabler, since leadership was so widely shared. Ken Solberg still seems to be the theological leader of the group, but he receives no salary, and there is no formal organizational dependence on him. The second decision reflects the informal organizational style of the group. Proceeding according to the dictum, "To grow, stay small," COACT split into two, then three house churches. Their separate identity was symbolized by separate worship services on Sunday evenings.

The group continues its growth and high activity level. Over 200 people have moved in and out of the group since its beginning, and there are now about 60 active members. Participants are involved in 24 different service projects in the larger community, and were very active in organizing for George McGovern in the 1972 Presidential race, winning four out of the five precincts they worked in. Task forces and support groups continue to form and disband as need and interest determine.

In the interview, the group articulated its purpose: "To free people to seek Christian lifestyles which express/result in personal growth, education, and outreach in social action." Specific goals focus on the tripartite program of the church: worship, education, and service. The characteristic language of the group balances interest in extended family human interaction, fun, and celebration with racial equality, Black empowerment, and political change.

COACT combines several frontiers of church renewal. Clergymen like to talk about being enablers, but few succeed in actually working themselves out of a job. Solberg's model of being a literal enabler, and perhaps moving on to form other groups, may be trend-setting. Second, the strong influence of human potential and organizational development disciplines helps COACT members combine skills in interpersonal relationships and community building with a focus on individual growth and awareness.

The human potential emphasis leads to a third trend-setting characteristic—the adoption of an organizational style that fits Warren Bennis's prediction that future institutions will be temporary systems.[3] People "flow in and out of COACT." Study groups and task forces form, work, and then disband rather than trying to achieve permanent existence. And even the group itself undergoes mitosis—splitting into two and then three separate house churches. Regardless of the rhetoric, the operational organizational style of most residential congregations is precisely the opposite—permanent membership, stable organizational form, resident paid staff. The COACT organizational style is what futurists like Alvin Toffler recommend. Is it a viable trend?

INTERPERSONAL RELATIONSHIPS

The second major way in which people relate to their religious community is by forming close friendships with other members. Responses to the study indicate that intimate relationships are quite a different motivation for and style of participation in a religious community than organizational activity. Love of neighbor has been expressed very differently in various communities of the Judaeo-Christian tradition. The implied intimacy of the report, "See how these christians love each other," is very different from the implied distance of sitting in a fixed pew for one hour a week in a large suburban congregation. In the latter case the sense of belonging to the church or synagogue may be quite significant in a person's life, but the fact of membership does not imply any need to be close to any other members of the group (with the possible exception of an important but structured relationship with the minister or rabbi).

In contemporary society many of the large organizations to which a person belongs have lost their credibility and clear significance. As "belonging" structures, to use William Schutz's term[4], they are less and less adequate to provide meaning and power for a person's life. As a result, there seems to be an increasing felt need for the experiences of close interpersonal relationships to fill the meaning gap. From psychoanalysis to encounter groups, many secondary institutions in modern culture are attempting to provide the experience of intimacy and to persuade persons that the experiences they offer are necessary and highly gratifying. Yet many churches and synagogues continue to build their programs around structures of more distant community, which meet the need for belonging but not the need for intimacy, adding supplemental structures like coffee hours or adult discussion groups to fill the gap. It is important to ask how much intimacy any person wants or can handle in his or her life, since intimacy requires the maturity and sense of identity to relate in spontaneous and vulnerable ways without a high level of anxiety. But in contemporary culture, intimacy is increasingly considered to be as one of the most important goals and experiences of life, if not the end of life itself. Institutions which offer such experiences and teach the skills to sustain closeness are in high demand.

Applying Schutz's distinction between belonging and affection, we attempted to distinguish the interpersonal relationship style of religious participation from that of organizational activity. We asked members of the groups a number of questions about the quality of their group's life and their motivations for participating in the group. The responses were factor analyzed, and the most important factor had to do with the positive quality of interpersonal relationships in the group, as follows:

TABLE III

Trust and Intimacy of Group Life

Can share my feelings in the group	.71
Encouraged to express my problems in the group	.68
Can fight for what I believe in without damaging group life	.64
Trust the others in the group	.57
Respected because of skills rather than office or length of membership	.52
Cooperate with members in group activities	.48

Several of these questions were clustered together on the questionnaire, and that may have affected their association in the factor. Nevertheless, the factor seems to represent a coherent set of judgments about the openness and intimacy of the group life as rated by the members. It does not say whether the member valued that intimacy as a motivation for belonging to the group, but whether it was present according to his or her perceptions. Conservative Protestants reported the most intimacy of this factor, followed by liberal Protestants, Jews, and others, with Roman Catholics last. These differences are significant to .014.

In their responses to the Rokeach list of instrumental values, participants in the study also indicated, at least with pencil and paper, their emphasis on interpersonal closeness.

The second factor of the Rokeach responses turned out as follows:

TABLE IV

Interpersonal Values

POSITIVE		NEGATIVE	
Forgiving	.75	Independent	−.49
Loving	.52	Logical	−.48
Cheerful	.50	Capable	−.42
Helpful	.47	Ambitious	−.38

This factor indicates a cluster of personality characteristics which value interpersonal intimacy and harmony over independent or competitive competencies to perform a task. Persons ranking high on this factor would logically seek a religious community emphasizing interpersonal closeness.

It is important to note that the motivation of interpersonal relationships is only loosely bound to institutions. If one joins a church or synagogue for intimacy, the organization which supports that network of relationships is only a means to an end, and not the goal itself. Therefore, if the religious institution does not provide sufficient opportunities for relationships or substitutes too much organizational maintenance activity for intimacy, persons seeking intimacy will rebel or leave. An example of a religious group that avoids this problem—one that is built very explicitly around the value of interpersonal relationships—is the Church of the Celebration.

The Church of the Celebration

The Church of the Celebration, in San Dimas, California, is an example of a church which focuses on personal growth and interpersonal intimacy. It uses sophisticated resources from humanistic psychology, and feels free to adapt or discard the traditional program and methods of the Church in the process. The church grew out of a series of role-play groups led by Bob Blees, now senior minister, at the request of the Southern California Yokefellows. In 1969, a nucleus of people who had participated in these growth groups decided that they wanted a "belonging" program as well as a "becoming" one. Under the aegis of the United Church of Christ, Bob Blees began an experimental ministry with this group, which formed as a community for continuing growth and social expression. Lay leadership developed within the group; the lay leaders received training and supervision, and lay-led groups were formed.

The group is now buying property from the United Church of Christ in San Dimas, where a traditional U.C.C. congregation failed. The sanctuary is used for everything from sleep-ins and musicals to monthly celebrations. The decision to buy the San Dimas property was a crossroads for the group in terms of group responsibility and individual commitment. As one member phrased it, "putting your money on the line was really putting yourself on the line."

The central feature of the church's life is role-playing workshops: through these workshops the church came into being, and through them new members enter the church. A workshop is like baptism, say the ministers—an initiatory rite. Once initiated, members continue to participate in role-playing workshops, through which members experience acceptance, discovering that it is all right to be themselves, and finding new ways of behaving and developing intimacy. Our researcher described her experience in the workshop:

I had a very exciting, happy time with the workshop. The members were very relaxed with one another and with me. They teased and laughed, and there was a great deal of hugging, men with men as well as with women. There was much openness about feelings; once they started sharing it was hard to stop them. Several talked about being "born" through this community. They all seemed to have gotten a great deal out of the workshop; the chance to reflect on who they were and to share in the meaning of the community seemed to be a new and important experience for them.

The program of the church also includes two monthly celebrations, which can take any shape from rock concert to poetry reading to personal sharing, one led by ministers, one by laity; quarterly "total involvement" live-in weekends; and individual counseling of group members by the ministers. One senses that the ministers' skills, vision, and commitment are central to the life of the group, although the ministers themselves are non-authoritarian, sharing their humanness with the members. Lay people initiate almost all programs. An elected board of trustees functions as a sounding board rather than a decision-making body.

The desire to facilitate personal growth is the primary motivating force behind the group's existence. The group describes its purpose in this way: "To be a community in which growth at your own pace and relationships are possible." Variations on this theme include the goals of self-acceptance, discovery, growth toward freedom, creativity, acceptance of others, nurturing the growth of others, and "knowing yourself as part of a vast creative process." One is struck by the strong emphasis on freedom, and the balance between freedom and responsibility; any person is free "to be" as long as that freedom does not limit the freedom of others. Despite their strong emphasis on relationship and responsibility, the community takes no group stand on social issues. The members can, and do, express individual concerns, but the group's primary emphasis is on respect for all points of view.

Though the ministers want the group to remain within the mainstream of Christianity, both ministers and lay people adamantly reject the need for creeds or beliefs as a condition for joining. Bob Blees, and some others, expressed a belief in a "vast unfolding process that one wants to tie into"—but some members wouldn't affirm even that. Other than the two monthly celebrations and the ministers' humanistically-oriented Bible study groups, there is almost nothing that reminds one of a church in the traditional sense. Members come from many groups—atheists, Buddhists, Jews, Catholics, Orthodox, mainline Protestants, and Mormons—and some still belong to other churches.

New members are recruited by word of mouth; as the minister says, "they select themselves." There are now about 350 participating members, including all ages and socio-economic backgrounds, ranging from professionals to blue-collar workers, students, and unemployed. Ninety percent of the members are white. Most come from within a 150-mile radius, but some come from all over the country to attend the workshops and join the community. They stay as long as their needs are met, moving on when they need to.

Eighty percent of the church budget is raised by the ministers through workshops, counseling and group fees, weddings, funerals, collections at services, etc. Members have pledged $1000 a month this year to buy the church property and to enable the ministers to continue to give as many free services as possible to the church.

There has been a good deal of discussion recently about declining local church budgets and membership, and the resulting surplus of clergy. One of the suggested solutions to this problem is "tent-making" ministers—clergy who make their living in secular positions, usually in the helping professions, and then contribute time to the leadership of the congregation. One difficulty with this solution is the role strain between secular occupation and congregational leadership. The Church of the Celebration offers another interesting alternative. The clergy do not depend for their living on exhortations to charitable giving. Instead, they receive fees for valued professional services and donate a significant portion of these fees to make a church community possible. Because of their commitment to encourage lay leadership, the ministers are not under pressure to assume the organizational leadership of the congregation as well. Their roles as ministers and as role-play leaders are well integrated and without conflict. At a time when the motivations for giving money are increasingly uncertain, the Church of the Celebration seems to offer a model worth testing for building a financially viable congregation.

PERSONAL RELIGIOUS EXPERIENCE AND DISCIPLINE

For many people, religion means experiencing the presence of God, and all else that religion implies must be added to this base. One clear finding of this report is the longing for authentic inner experience. Religious groups that tend to influence our changing culture and to facilitate a more humane society must take this hunger seriously.

Those who value personal religious experience and discipline, like those who value interpersonal relationships, treat the religious organization as a means to their end.

We refer here to experience *and* discipline since there is evidence that people in some traditions understand relationship with God to be a matter of discipline, while people in other traditions understand it to be a matter of experience. People who receive their primary values through belonging to an institution may understand discipline as the way to the experience of God, while those who primarily evolve their values from their own experience tend to regard the careful nurturing of inner experience itself as the way to the Spirit.

There were a number of indicators in the study of participants' valuing religious experience and discipline. The questions on affiliation with church or synagogue produced a second factor which positively valued personal discipline and de-emphasized organizational participation.

TABLE V

Personal Religious Discipline

POSITIVE		NEGATIVE	
Frequency of prayer	.52	Self-rating of activity in	
Frequency of talking		church or synagogue	−.56
about religion with		Frequency of attending	
friend or co-workers	.48	meetings	−.46
Frequency of reading			
Bible	.41		

On this factor the Catholics in the study ranked highest, followed by conservative Protestants, others, and liberal Protestants, with Jews last. Here people in "other" religious groups show more interest in personal religious experience and discipline than do either liberal Protestants or Jews. These differences are statistically significant beyond .001. Participants also responded to a series of questions asking about the occurrence of "profound inner experience, such as joy, serenity, peace, inspiration, or mystical feeling," and about having strong religious beliefs and convictions. On both of these scales the various traditions ranked in the same order: conservative Protestants highest, followed by Roman Catholics, liberal Protestants, other groups, and Jews. (One of the five Jewish groups represented secular Judaism, making the Jewish rank lower than it might otherwise have been.) These differences are statistically significant beyond .001.

While conservative Protestants and Roman Catholics in the study rank highest on these measures of personal religious experience and discipline, the hunger for that experience is certainly not confined to them. It may be that liberal Protestants have most misunderstood the needs of their people and discouraged rather than nurtured this need. Because that hunger for personal religious experience is so widespread, and so many different groups are responding to it, it is instructive to look at Tail of the Tiger, a Tibetan Buddhist community whose central activity is meditation.

Tail of the Tiger

Tail of the Tiger is a meditative community in Barnet, Vermont, dedicated to understanding and following the teachings of Tibetan Buddhism. It began in May, 1970, under the leadership of Chogyam Trungpa Rimpoche, the eleventh incarnation of the Trungpa Tulka and abbot of a group of Tibetan monasteries. At the age of nineteen, he led a party of refugees out of Tibet to escape the persecution of the Chinese Communists. The Vermont community owes it formation and its life to Rimpoche, who is a spiritual guide, or, as he prefers to call himself, "a spiritual friend" to all the members. He emphasizes relating the teachings of Tibetan Buddhism to the specific circumstances of American life. Such concerns of Americans as "sex, work, and money" are addressed from the perspective of the fundamental teaching of Buddha, namely, the understanding of the four marks of existence: impermanence *(anitya),* suffering *(dukha),* void *(shunyata),* and egolessness *(anata).*

The group, which lives on a farm, now has 24 permanent members. There are three meditation periods each day, and members are encouraged to go on month-long retreats. A shrine room and craft center have been built, and the community publishes an occasional journal.

The community is organized informally. The group meets every morning and work assignments are made by volunteering, or by group pressure when necessary. The pressure, however, is not heavy-handed. The community governs itself, subject to Rimpoche's direction when he is present. For example, community members combine an easy corporate democracy with the guru's direct personal authority in their individual lives. One girl recounted how she had come to the community during a vacation and then decided to stay as a permanent member until, as she said, "Rimpoche says, 'Do something else.' " The community is impressive physically in its cleanliness, orderliness, and good repair of the buildings.

At the end of 1970, Rimpoche founded a second community, Karma Dzong, outside of Boulder, Colorado, which caused some mistrust and sense of rivalry on the part of the Vermont community.

During the interview, the group had a great deal of difficulty with the word "goal," since it implies an attachment to worldly pursuits that is the opposite of Buddhist aims. The group insisted that members are individuals and that the group as such has only practical goals, such as making the community self-sufficient and building new cabins. The group articulated its purpose variously as "Rimpoche," "incorporate Tibetan teachings into American life," "practice in meditation." For each person the goal is the path itself, wherever one happens to be on the path. Explicit goals of spiritual growth are a sign of ambition or "spiritual materialism" and a misunderstanding of Tibetan Buddhism. Each person is involved in an evolutionary growth process in which, as one person put it, "everything we are (potentially) is already contained in the seed we are now."

One person claimed that most members are still involved in personal "trips," and have not yet begun to work seriously with the teachings of Tibetan Buddhism.

Although there are no goals in the ultimate sense, and even all practical goals are empty *(sunya),* there are still concerns of the community and steps for the individual to follow. The community is concerned about becoming more rigorous in its Tibetan Buddhist disciplines. Members also want "interviews" with Rimpoche for spiritual advice when he is at the farm. One of the frustrations of the community is that he is not always with them. During the group interview, a group fantasy was generated. In it, one member suggested that the community would build a nice house for Rimpoche just down the road and "he would live there all the time."

The characteristic language of the community reflects the general teachings of Tibetan Buddhism as interpreted by Rimpoche. "Cutting through" refers to stripping away the bonds of ego-attachment; "tripping out" or "neurotic" means preoccupation with ego satisfactions. "Idiot compassion" is Rimpoche's term for easy sentimentality as exemplified by the feigned fellowship of encounter groups, or the avoidance of hard decisions.

The relationships in the group attempt the same rigor. The group is together because of mutual interest in Tibetan Buddhism, not because of warm feelings for one another. The researcher noted that the group "refuses to be seduced into being nice and friendly" to each other or to outsiders. However, there is a good deal of fun and closeness in the group, though little touching. Outsiders are neither excluded nor welcomed. The group uses a good deal of humor, some of it self-directed, against taking oneself or one's spiritual path too seriously. One person said, "nothing is to be taken seriously, save the teachings and death"—certainly not the ego nor one's own earnestness. The researcher concluded about the group: "They have a feeling of correctness about what they are doing."

Many commentators have remarked on the increasing appeal of Eastern religions to many people in our culture. According to Needleman in *The New Religions,* this appeal is due to their ability to offer practical methods of growth, enlightenment, or salvation.[5] Liberal Protestant churches especially have offered few specific, workable, and interesting disciplines that people could adopt for their own growth. One of the members summed up this dimension of the attractiveness of Tail of the Tiger: "The only thing that makes us any different, the only thing that makes us an alternative, is that we do meditate. That's the one really hopeful thing."

The group has interesting implications for the role and function of the ministry and rabbinate as well. In psychoanalytic thought, "transference" is the irrational projection onto the therapist of unconscious conflicts in the patient, and the attempt to resolve those conflicts through the relationship itself. This concept gives all therapists who follow the psychoanalytic model a clear understanding of the place their relationship with the patient plays in the therapeutic process. Tail of the Tiger has an equally clear understanding of the relationship of the guru to the seeker, and the place that this relationship plays in the process of spiritual enlightenment. The relationship is a matter of profound emotion and exists whether or not the two are physically present. In a curious and intriguing analogy to the way the therapist works with transference, the guru both invites and frustrates the relationship. Both guru and follower understand that the seeker will attempt to shortcut the arduous process of spiritual growth through a dependency relationship and by attempting to manipulate the guru into magically bestowing spiritual maturity upon him/her. Therefore, the guru both intrigues the disciple along the path through the relationship and, as one of the members put it, "continually disappoints our expectations." Hopefully the disciple eventually learns to take sole responsibility for finding a personal spiritual path.

Many priests, ministers, and rabbis have no such clear concept of the role their relationship plays in the spiritual growth of parishioners. Instead, many feel restricted by traditional definitions and forms, neither finding the original meaning behind them nor developing alternatives as clear and intentional as are those of the psychoanalyst or of Rimpoche.

The final implication of this group for the study is the alternative doctrine of salvation it presents. It bears interesting relationships to such recent theological fashions as the death of God, but in its rigor and seriousness it is more impressive. Why is it that these seemingly alien systems of thought take powerful root in the lives of persons in our culture? Eastern disciplines may offer a helpful challenge and even a source of renewal to the Judaeo-Christian tradition in the process.

THE IMPORTANCE OF CHARISMA

We used a variety of data analysis processes in addition to the ones reported above to see what we could learn about the groups that might suggest appropriate planning for churches and synagogues. One very important conclusion that emerged from the data analysis is the importance of a strong leader(s) for the life of these groups. It isn't news to suggest that behind most religious groups stands the vision and leadership abilities of specific men and women, but it is important to understand the significance of this leadership for the groups' vitality. Some groups were founded around the charisma of a particular person who has remained the central figure, like Rev. Charlotte Baker of King's Temple. In other cases, part of the vision of the founder was to enable a community, and then intentionally remove himself or herself from the leadership position, as was true for Rev. Ken Solberg of COACT. In other instances, the group needed to go through a wrenching struggle over purpose and program in order to arrive at a clear identity and leadership, as happened with St. Francis Presbyterian Church. In still other examples, the history of the group may have been scarred by continuing power struggles over leadership, which was the case with Emmaus House. But in many cases, myth and community were the expression of a vision originally resident in one human being. What seems to be needed is a clarity and energy or enthusiasm in the leader about a vision of mission and community. The community's formation around the vision depends on the organizing skills and energy of the leader. The vision can remain very much the leader's vision, in which followers participate, or it can be taken over and transmuted by the community in the course of its history. Urban Holmes, in *The Future Shape of Ministry,* suggests that the Christian minister should be a "sacramental person,"[6] who in his own life and work transmits to others the personal revelation of God in Jesus Christ. The charismatic leader is a person who both forms and is formed by a larger vision which he or she communicates in everyday acts of living and being. The communication is as idiosyncratic as the particular interests, abilities, and personality characteristics of each leader, and may be as grand and powerful as the vision of God that has seized him or her. Because charisma is so much a function of the unique personality of the leader, it is difficult to make general statements about it. And for the same reason it is even more difficult to suggest how charismatic leaders can be 'trained' or formed for the renewal of churches and synagogues. One is tempted to fall back upon such clichés as 'good leaders are born, not made.' But there are skills and insights from the social sciences, management training, psychotherapy, the human potential movement, and other disciplines that can greatly help leaders to be more effective. And in fact, some of the groups in the study, such as COACT, and St. Francis Presbyterian Church made liberal use of such resources for the growth of the community, and, it may be presumed, for the growth of the leadership. Still, the vision itself is more caught than taught. Here the selection process is at least as important as the training process, as Holmes suggests. Ways need to be found to identify and nurture those leaders who already have a vision, and are already community forming persons, whether they be professional religious leaders, or volunteers. Among the groups in the study, at times the leadership was not from professionals but from lay persons from many different walks of life who had in common only the vision of faith and community and the charisma to share it effectively.

The dependence on the charismatic leader is particularly striking in the Jewish groups in the study.

Rabbi Steven Riskin of Lincoln Square Synagogue in New York City offers an interesting example of the power of charismatic leadership.

Lincoln Square Synagogue

Located in the Lincoln Square area of New York City, a complex of upper-middle class apartments, Lincoln Square Synagogue held its first Sabbath service in December, 1964, in an apartment house, with 15 people in attendance. In 1965, Steven Riskin, an Orthodox rabbi, came to the synagogue, and the membership rose to 75 families. The rapid growth in membership and activity made it impossible to continue holding Sabbath services in the apartment house. Members also wanted to find an alternative to holding High Holidays at the Riverside Plaza Hotel. They made a commitment to build their own synagogue. Though the first fund raising drive failed, a second drive carried out by the members raised enough money to begin the new building. Under Riskin's leadership, the synagogue has grown to 350 family members and 150 individual adult members. Even with the new building, members have to arrive at services early in order to get a seat. In the congregation there are a few more women than men. Forty percent of the congregation is under 35, while thirty percent are over 65. The synagogue is supported by dues—families pay $100 a year, single persons $50, with High Holy Day tickets extra. The staff has grown until now there are two rabbis, a cantor, and twenty part-time faculty persons for the Hebrew schools.

The basic direction of the synagogue has been toward traditional Jewish orthodoxy. According to Orthodox law, men and women are separated in the service. Instead of reducing the amount of Jewish law and tradition which needs to be taught, Lincoln Square Synagogue insists upon the full tradition as necessary and relevant to the lives of the congregants. One member said in the group interview that his most meaningful experience since he had been with the synagogue was being chosen to hold the Torah during one of the services. During the service he experienced "the sense of continuity in Judaism," feeling himself part of a tradition which goes back thousands of years.

From the beginning, the program has been built around intensive adult education classes. In 1972 there were twenty-six separate courses offered during the year, attended by approximately 800 people. In addition to the adult education program, which is called the Joseph Shapiro Academy, there is a nursery for preschool children, a religious school for primary school children, and a Hebrew high school. During the discussion of education, the interview group affirmed the basic identity or purpose of the synagogue as "Torah Education," education around Jewish thought, Jewish living, Jewish lifestyle, Jewish values. The first specific goal the group articulated was "to achieve and maintain Jewish survival." Jewish survival depends upon the return to the traditions and the reawakening of Jewish consciousness through Torah study. The congregation identifies itself with a progressive, orthodox Judaism "retaining the full content of the law, but adapting to modern forms." The rabbi is open to any manner of modern technology in the service of Torah education, from advertising in the *Times* to renting a parking lot in order to make the Succah available, because the synagogue facilities are not large enough for all who wish it. In order to enable the community, including non-members, to participate, the synagogue remodeled a truck into a "Succah On Wheels."

Completed in 1971 at a cost of $1,200,000, the synagogue is built around the vision of Rabbi Riskin. The sanctuary seats over 500 people in an intimate setting in the round, with circular, tiered seats. Members believe that the atmosphere communicates the rabbi's vision of a close and caring community. It is comfortable, intimate, and as one said, "somewhat expensive." The congregation's enthusiastic singing is due, according to the cantor, not to his own leading but to the enthusiasm of the rabbi, who by his clapping (and even jumping) during the singing encourages members to sing joyfully before the Lord.

The synagogue is built around the charismatic leadership of Rabbi Riskin, who combines an extraordinary ability to elicit love, admiration, and devotion from his followers with unusual skill in teaching the Jewish tradition. He has initiated and encouraged a wide variety of lay participation in the life of the synagogue, and developed a community in which people seem to care very much for one another. Members speak of the love the rabbi has for them, and in un-self-conscious ways of their love for and devotion to him. The assistant rabbi said that Riskin calls up absentees after the service out of his concern for them. One member said, "The rabbi is like a mother to us." For another, the most important experience he had had since joining the synagogue was eating at the rabbi's table and experiencing how the rabbi related to his own family as a Jew.

Members said that as a teacher, "the rabbi learns with us," expounding the tradition "with crystal clarity," not as dead law, but as religious experience. According to Rabbi Riskin, "One of the most unique aspects of Judaism is the fact that the intellectual pursuit of Torah study plays a primary role in the religious experience."

One member characterized the synagogue as "short on planning and great on improvisation." The rabbi, a creative leader, often gets spur-of-the-moment ideas, and presses both staff and lay members into these new projects. The assistant said, "We do what he wants us to do because we love him. It's a funny thing; we get involved in what he is doing and we think we are going to save the world." "There is never such a thing as the word 'impossible,'" according to one member. The rabbi becomes convinced that something needs to be done, and it is done, whether or not it seems impossible in terms of time, money, or other problems. Two persons summed up the group's feelings about Steven Riskin during the group interview: "The rabbi is something that God has given to us."

Other goals of the Lincoln Square community include reaching out to uncommitted Jews and bringing them into the synagogue, making people more knowledgeable about the Jewish tradition, building a strong Jewish institution to influence both the American value system and the State of Israel. Still another goal is to help Rabbi Riskin realize his potential and his mission.

These goals form an integrated whole around the basic purpose of the group. During the group interview, members described the growth of Jewish consciousness in their own lives. "Care," "love," and "concern" are the important words in the common life of the synagogue, along with "Shabbos Services," "the Wednesday night lectures," and "community" *(Kehillah).*

We have examined the major concerns of the religious communities in the study and the styles of group participation of members and leaders. We now turn our attention in more detail to the people who actually comprise the groups we have been studying—the group members themselves.

5

The People Who Belong

GRADS, NOT DROP-OUTS

What sort of people find their way into these religious communities? Are they strangers to church and synagogue life? Are they drop-outs from religious groups, or graduates of them? We found that members of the groups studied are more knowledgeable on matters of religion than the average member of a church or synagogue. The questionnaire used the items of biblical knowledge developed by Charles Glock and Rodney Stark.[1] On all items the mean scores of respondents were higher than those of the Glock and Stark sample, and in almost all items, significantly higher. These and other data lead to the conclusion that the persons in the study do not differ in belief and behavior from average members of the three faiths out of ignorance of those traditions. Instead, they seem to be more like graduates of the traditional religious groups. They have learned and practiced the faith, and in many cases they have found their way into positions of leadership and have given long service. If these people now struggle to find new symbols to express their faith, or experiment with novel communities that do not fit into established institutions, it may not be because traditional communities have failed. It may be because they did too

83

good a job. Having known the best of the present, these graduates may be leading the way into the future.

THEIR RELIGIOUS EXPERIENCE

How do persons in these groups experience the presence of God? For most, formal worship is not the most important source of religious experiences. One hundred thirteen respondents mentioned being with friends as the source of religious experience, 76 mentioned prayer or meditation, 45 specified church or synagogue worship or the sacraments, and 43 listed the experience of nature as the occasion of religious experience. Sixteen persons referred to reading Scripture and 10 to a drug experience. The religious experiences reported were usually specific events, not just vague feelings. Of 275 responses which could be coded, 72 percent described experiences happening in a definite time and place. We also found that two-thirds of the respondents said they prayed once a day or more. This high frequency of prayer among non-traditional groups has been confirmed in other studies. It suggests that the term "prayer" has a variety of meanings, and does not simply refer to the traditional formal verbal prayers in a worship service or at a stated time. Of 332 responses, 68 described prayer in traditional terms, 18 described meditation, and 15 referred to specific non-traditional methods such as journal writing. Forty-seven persons expressed negative attitudes toward traditional prayer.

The actual religious experiences of group members vary. One hundred and six persons described their experience as a conversion, a definite turning point or salvation. Ninety-three responses were about a continuity of experience, e.g., a journey or path, gradual growth, or learning. One hundred and forty-seven responses used the current language of expansion of consciousness, or new awareness.

For most persons in the study, then, religious experience is a personal event unrelated to the formal liturgies of church and synagogue where people traditionally expect to experience the presence of God.

THEIR RELIGIOUS BELIEFS AND LANGUAGE

Jeffrey Hadden and other researchers have remarked about the erosion of traditional beliefs and traditional religious language.[2] Martin Marty, in an unpublished paper reflecting on our data, remarks that "there is a pluralist, Protean, palimpsestic character to ideology: people absorb various competitive signals. The Jesus freak, prodded, often admits to being also a believer in astral projection and reincarnation; the renewed nuns read Christian Scriptures aloud while showing a quiet film about a Buddhist monk novice."[3] The people in this study show both the loss of traditional religious language, and the use of pluralistic, even contradictory excerpts from various myths and belief systems in order to interpret their own experience.

We asked people to tell us in their own words if they had had what they would call religious experiences, and if so, with what situations or events they were usually associated. The "religious" experiences reported ranged from the felt presence of divinity described in orthodox language to events of everyday life described without the use of any religious language whatsoever. Eighty-seven persons experienced the personal presence of, or personal relationship with, the Christian or Jewish divinity. But 157 persons reported as religious experiences the experiencing of their own selves as whole, authentic, or autonomous.

This last finding indicates, perhaps more clearly than any other, the loss of the traditional language of the Judaeo-Christian myths and the search for adequate symbols to express the sacred events of life. From an orthodox Christian or Jewish perspective, it is the God of creation and history who alone is worthy of worship, not one's own self. Yet for significant numbers of people, the experience of self as whole is a sacred event, tapping the same dimensions of awe and love that for most Christians and Jews is only appropriate to the worship of the living God as He has revealed Himself. Here we are on difficult and dangerous ground. Some would understand this phenomenon as evidence of the urgent need to preach the saving knowledge of God to these persons who are in darkness. Others would understand it as evidence of the loss of potency of Judaeo-Christian language in our time, and a struggle for symbols that make better sense of current personal experience. Carl Jung would have understood it as the emergence of the archetype of the Self.[4] Serious theological work is needed to understand these honest and sometimes poignant reports of human experience of the sacred. A wide variety of special terminologies was used to describe religious experiences and beliefs and values. Many people used words from several different fields in a single response, evidence that their values are a synthesis of convictions from several myth-bearing communities. Only a few orthodox or evangelical groups stayed within one language system, even to the point of rejecting questionnaire items which used words outside the system. As for frequency patterns, people in the study used humanistic language most often, followed by traditional Christian, liberal Christian, evangelical Christian, and Jewish Orthodox terms. It is interesting that explicitly psychological language was seldom used.

ETHICAL BELIEFS

To the extent that ethical beliefs can be indicated by pencil and paper instruments, we have some interesting data on what Milton Rokeach terms the "instrumental values" of persons in the study.[5] Using Rokeach's questionnaire, we asked each interviewee to rank the following list of values in order of importance in his/her own life:

ambitious	forgiving	logical
broadminded	helpful	loving
capable	honest	obedient
cheerful	imaginative	polite
clean	independent	responsible
courageous	intellectual	self-controlled

This approach has the disadvantage of furnishing present categories to which the person must respond and therefore perhaps elicits formal value statements rather than a description of the valuing or choosing processes a person actually uses. But it has the advantage of having been used nationally, giving us some comparisons with the general population. The responses of our participants to the list of values is compared in the following table, with the national samples developed by Rokeach. The similarities and differences are very much worth noting. Overall, "honest" and "loving" are the values most important to people in the study. "Broadminded" is next. The national sample agrees in ranking "honest" first, but puts "loving" way down the list for Protestants and Catholics, and puts "ambitious" in second place. Only Jews rank "broadminded" as high as the persons in the study.

At the bottom of the list respondents ranked "obedient" with "polite," and "clean" only slightly more valued. The national sample rates "obedience" a little more favorably and "polite" and "clean" much more favorably. At the bottom of the list for Protestants and Catholics is "imaginative." Again, Jews are closest to our respondents, also ranking "obedient" last.

TABLE VI

Instrumental Values

Comparison of Members' Rankings with Rankings of National Sample

	PROTESTANTS NATIONALLY	PROTESTANTS IN STUDY	ROMAN CATHOLICS NATIONALLY	ROMAN CATHOLICS IN STUDY	JEWS NATIONALLY	JEWS IN STUDY
1. Ambitious	2	13	2	16	6	14
2. Broadminded	5	3	6	6	2	7
3. Capable	11	9	8	10	5	4
4. Cheerful	12	11	10	8	10	13
5. Clean	8	17	9	18	11	17
6. Courageous	6	16	5	7	17	6
7. Forgiving	4	7	4	3	15	11
8. Helpful	7	5	7	5	9	5
9. Honest	1	2	1	1	1	3
10. Imaginative	18	8	18	11	17	9
11. Independent	14	10	14	9	3	10
12. Intellectual	16	12	17	12	8	8
13. Logical	17	15	15	13	12	12
14. Loving	10	1	11	2	14	1
15. Obedient	15	18	16	17	18	17
16. Polite	13	16	13	15	16	16
17. Responsible	3	4	3	4	4	2
18. Self-controlled	9	14	9	14	3	15

Note: These figures are based on 227 responses.

Members of the groups studied show very high interest in loving relationships, in contrast to the population at large. There is less devotion to ambition—which suggests an openness to less competitive lifestyles. The low ranking of obedience and politeness suggests an interest in collegially-oriented and informal organizations and decision-making structures, which in fact characterize many of the groups studied. Finally, the high value placed on honesty by both the sample and the general population points to an area in which these groups can make contact with the generally accepted values of Americans.

CONCERN FOR PERSONAL GROWTH

In addition to questions about religious beliefs and values, we also asked people about their general life concerns. What appeared was a strong interest in their own personal growth and character development, in contrast to the concerns of the general population. Using the instrument developed by Hadley Cantril, members were asked the following general question:

All of us want certain things out of life. When you think about what really matters in your own life, what are your wishes and hopes for the future? In other words, if you imagine your future in the *best* possible light what would your life look like then, if you are to be happy?[6]

They were then asked the opposite question, to describe the worst possible life for them. Cantril's own coding system was used to score the data, in order to make comparisons with the general population possible.

Persons in this study most often listed wishes for their own personal character, and secondly, wishes for their family. In describing their best possible life, the respondents listed concerns about their own personal character a total of 382 times. Chief among these concerns were self-development or improvement, often in religious terms, and a desire for acceptance by others. Second most frequent in descriptions of the best possible life were references to the person's family (181 responses). Eighty-two percent of those responses mentioned a happy family life. These concerns offer an interesting contrast to those of the general population, as shown in the following chart.

TABLE VII

Rankings of Concerns of Persons in Groups Studied with
Concerns of General Population
(Concerns listed in order of frequency)

GROUPS STUDIED	GENERAL POPULATION
1. personal character: self-development, acceptance by others, resolution of religious problems, sense of personal worth, emotional stability	1. health
2. happy family	2. decent standard of living
	3. children
	4. housing
	5. happy family

The same concern for self-development or improvement emerged when respondents described their fears of the worst imaginable life.

TABLE VIII

Rankings of Fears of Persons in Groups Studied with Fears of
General Population
(Fears listed in order of frequency)

GROUPS STUDIED	GENERAL POPULATION
1. own personal character: lack of self-development, not accepted, no self-worth	1. own health difficulty
2. other references to self: own health difficulty, separation from God	2. family health difficulty

There was some resistance among evangelical groups to describing a worst possible life. That task seemed to some to be a tempting of God, a denial of trust in His goodness and providence in caring for the believer. A few refused even to describe a best possible life on the grounds that one should not make plans, but simply trust in God's leading. The survey reveals high interest among members of these groups in personal development or growth and personal experiences of peace and emotional stability, in contrast to the chief concerns of the general population. Methods of personal growth and spiritual experience should clearly have a wide appeal to members of these groups. The promise of finding such opportunities was probably an important factor in their joining and participating in religious groups. But second only to this concern for personal growth was the concern for their families, and on the negative side, the fear of not being accepted. This interest in interpersonal closeness shows up again and again among the members of these groups.

CONCERN FOR PERSONAL SECURITY

A coherent cluster of responses to the study emerged around what can be called a concern for one's own personal security, i.e., the sense that one's physical and psychic survival and well being are reasonably well assured. Religious traditions minister to these needs in many different ways, but neglect them at peril to their institutional life. Persons in this study indicated that personal security is important to them, and perhaps constitutes part of their motivation for belonging to the religious groups studied. The imperative to love God and neighbor is interpreted by various religious groups to sanction some of these needs, but not others. For example, in the Judaeo-Christian tradition, most groups teach that loving one's neighbor as oneself implies some self-denial in order to serve others. But judgments about which needs are denied and which are to be met vary from group to group.

There seem to be two main areas of individual security values. The first has to do with the outward necessities—in this culture, an adequate income, a good job, decent housing, a secure and reasonably happy family life. We call these "environmental security values" and used the Cantril instrument described above to measure their importance for the participants.

Questionnaire responses were subjected to factor analysis. The first factor on the responses to the Cantril instrument seemed to indicate five types of environmental security values (Table IX). The higher the numbers, the more closely associated the item is with the factor itself.

TABLE IX

Environmental Security Values of Members of Groups Studied

Hopes for a good, steady, congenial or successful job .694
Fears about lack of family or children or with
    threats to health or life of family or children .646

Hopes for happy or healthy family and children   .585
Fears about poor or uncongenial job, unemployment,
   or failure in work   .520
Hopes for improved or decent standard of living   .450

The second major category of individual security values can be called "psychic security values." In addition to their need for a supporting environment, human beings also seem to have a fundamental aspiration to mature, to fulfill their potential for growth. Abraham Maslow has posited that human beings have a hierarchy of needs, starting at the bottom in the needs for physical survival and ending at the top in the aspiration to realize the fullness of one's human potential.[7] This second category of individual security values is on the lower part of the ladder of psychological needs—the desire for psychological security rather than the desire for psychic growth.

The first indicator of psychic security values comes from the Cantril category of fears about one's own personal character, including fears of emotional instability, of not being accepted by others, or fear of lacking a sense of personal worth. We also used a personality inventory in the study which includes six scales relating to psychic security needs.[8] It should be emphasized that the scales were not used to measure the psychic health of the persons in the study—a dubious enterprise at best—but to indicate the extent to which persons in the various groups hold psychic security values and are encouraged to hold them by the teaching of their religious tradition. For example, one of the scales asks persons if they are disturbed by socially unacceptable impulses. Liberal Protestants with a fair degree of psychological awareness might tend to answer no to such a question because their value system does not sanction a yes response. Either they have learned that "everyone" has socially unacceptable impulses and not to be disturbed by them, or they believe themselves to have attained such a level of psychological health that such impulses are no longer present. A conservative Protestant, on the other hand, might tend to answer yes to the same question because the psyche is understood to be a battleground between the spirit of God and the spirit of evil, and socially unacceptable impulses are to be fought against by faith.

SOCIAL CONCERNS

We asked persons to share their concerns about the society in which they live. The results indicate a critical but optimistic attitude toward the society, and specific interests in working for social change.

For example, we asked participants what they believed about the American way of life. Of 345 persons, only one-fourth consider the American way of life superior or good. For slightly over half (53%), it is bad or at best ambivalent. One-fifth believe it to be good as an ideal but corrupted in practice. Domestic social problems are most often mentioned in describing its shortcomings. One-half believe some change is needed in institutions in society and one-third that a complete reform or overhaul from within is needed. Only 8% believe in the necessity for revolution, and only 8% believe change is not possible. In fact, almost everyone, 337 out of 338 responses, believed that change was good, with some adding the restriction that it be appropriately or religiously guided. There is nothing else on which respondents agree so much as on the desirability of change.

In order to find out specifically what they wished to change, we used a card sort in which persons in the survey were asked to separate out the cards representing areas in which they wished to see change and were in fact presently working for change. Areas listed covered everything from personal health to the Federal Government. Four blank cards were included to allow people to fill in concerns not already listed on other cards. The first important finding was the sheer number of concerns. Of 351 persons using the cards, 142 listed at least 21 areas in which they saw a need for change. Cards were re-sorted so that respondents could list areas in which they not only saw the need for change, but were presently working to bring about changes. The most frequently listed areas in which people had specific commitments were: schools or education (140 persons); culture or society's values (114); peace (105); ecology or conservation (96); personal religious faith (89); racism (87); and police, courts, prisons (83).

In the Cantril questionnaire, concerns for the social order emerged as the second most important category (or factor) of concerns after personal security issues.

TABLE X

Concerns for Social Order of Members of Groups Studied

Fears of social injustice	.783
Fears of lack of freedom, no improvement in government	.726
Hopes for social justice	.706
Fear of war, militarism, foreign powers	.605

The findings indicate then that persons in these religious groups tend to be concerned about the social order and are willing to work to improve it.

OPTIMISM

Finally, participants in the study are a little more optimistic about the future generally, and about organized religion in particular, than the general population. On the Cantril instrument, persons were asked to consider a ten point scale, or ladder. If the best possible life, as they themselves have described it, is ten on the ladder, and their own description of the worst possible life is zero, where would they consider themselves now, five years ago, and five years from now. The members of the religious groups studied are more optimistic about the past, present, and especially the future than the general population.

TABLE XI

Comparative Self-Ratings of Group Members with Self-Ratings of General Population[8]

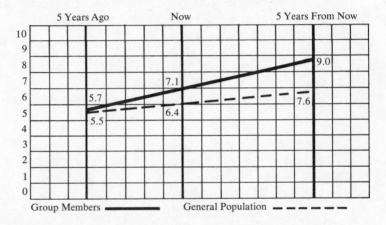

| 5 Years Ago | Now | 5 Years From Now |

Group Members ━━━━━   General Population ━ ━ ━ ━ ━

They are also more optimistic about the influence of religion in this culture. According to the Gallup Poll, 75% of Americans think that the influence of religion is decreasing, and only 14% think it is increasing. In contrast, 47% of respondents to the study believe religion is decreasing in influence, and 36% think it is becoming more influential.[9]

The groups we studied count thousands of people among their members—people who share many of the same beliefs, concerns, and attitudes. What we have learned about these communities and their members should say something to persons concerned about the vitality of institutional religion in our culture.

Religious Vitality: Conservative and Liberal

If the groups we have studied are examples of the vitality of American religious life, what do they suggest about the future of organized religion? Keeping in mind that these groups are only a sample of what a panel of religious leaders considered to be vital communities, what clues do they offer to those concerned about the future of religion in a changing culture?

CONSERVATIVE CHURCHES ARE NOT THE ONLY ONES THAT ARE GROWING

In the first chapter, we summarized the evidence that organized religion, as measured by such indicators as membership and financial contributions, was no longer growing as it had in the 1950's, and in some cases was actually declining. However, conservative Protestant churches were continuing to grow while liberal Protestant churches were declining in institutional strength.

Dean Kelley, in *Why Conservative Churches Are Growing,* argued that this differential demonstrated that conservative churches are meeting the personal need for meaning in contemporary society more adequately than the liberal churches. He defined religion as "the human enterprise by which a sacred cosmos is established." A "sacred cosmos," following Berger and Luckmann's work, is a system of fundamental meaning believed to underlie and organize the universe; it is a perspective from which to view and understand reality. Kelley went on to say that it is the sacred cosmos that provides humans with their ultimate shield against the terror of anomie, the absence of values and guides for life. Regardless of what else it does, religion must carry and transmit a sacred cosmos for people. The Church is a social phenomenon providing in the interaction of the group a set of meanings, or at least an atmosphere which is conducive to the search for meaning.[1]

In contemporary pluralistic society, the institutions which touch our lives do not provide a consistent meaning structure. These institutions present a myriad number of conflicting value structures that force the individual to establish his or her own value system. Therefore, the search for meaning is more difficult than ever in contemporary society because one can no longer depend on an integrated society to provide us with a consistent set of meanings.

The church or synagogue, as a result, stands as a beacon because it provides a sacred cosmos or comprehensive set of values. It was Kelley's thesis that conservative churches, since they provide clear-cut, unambiguous, and authoritative sets of values, were meeting contemporary man's need for meaning more adequately than the liberal churches. He developed six characteristics which distinguish the conservative churches from the liberal churches:

ABSOLUTISM——the belief that one's own particular group has the truth and that all others are in error, comprising a closed system of meaning and value which explains everything; an uncritical and unreflective attachment to a single set of values.

CONFORMITY——an intolerance of any dissent or deviance which constitutes a threat to the values of the group. This implies a separatist stance in relation to other groups.

DISCIPLINE——the willingness to obey commands without question and to suffer sanctions for infractions rather than leave the group.

COMMITMENT——the willingness to sacrifice status for the cause of the group and for group solidarity; the total identification of the individual's goals with the group's goals.

MISSIONARY ZEAL——the eagerness to tell the good news of one's experience.

FANATICISM——relating to other persons and groups by the strategies of "Flood (all talk and no listen) or isolation (keep yourselves unspotted from the world)."[2]

Kelley concluded from case studies of some religious movements in history and from such denominational statistics as membership and financial contributions that "strong groups" are groups which have the six characteristics he described. The argument rests on the assumption that such indicators as membership and financial contributions are the primary indicators of a "strong group."

The groups in our study present a much more complex picture than can be dealt with by Kelley's analysis. They were nominated by religious leaders because they seemed to be providing the meaning-laden experiences that Kelley believes to be the essential function of religion. But they are providing those experiences in ways that cut across the categories of his analysis. If the indicators of "strong groups" are growth in membership and financial contributions, then liberal groups like Glide, COACT, and Church of the Celebration are growing as well as conservative churches such as King's Temple and Prince of Peace. In addition, some groups, such as Solel Synagogue and COACT, deliberately eschewed membership growth as the indicator of their vitality either by refusing to accept new members beyond a certain number, or by splitting into new smaller groups when more than a certain number of persons joined. Finally, Kelley's six categories (absolutism, etc.) simply do not apply to some of the growing conservative churches in the study, such as Prince of Peace.

CONVENTIONAL AND INDIVIDUATED VALUES

We do believe, however, that there is an important distinction between two fundamental ways in which religious communities attempt to meet the need for meaning in contemporary life. Kelley's categories perhaps point to this distinction, but do not properly identify it. We prefer the terms "conventional and individuated values," adapting the polarity from a study by Wentzel of Presbyterian, Baptist, and Catholic congregations.[3] Wentzel found that the first factor emerging from the analysis of his questionnaire results was what he termed "conventional" versus "liberal" values. This polarity has important implications for understanding the growth of conservative churches in comparison to liberal groups. As we use the terms in this study, conventional and individuated values are two basically different ways by which persons choose and act, or value, in their daily lives. Religious groups teach, and persons tend to live their lives, somewhere on a continuum between the two poles of conventional and individuated values. The poles may be defined as follows:

Conventional values are received on the authority of the religious tradition or fundamental social structure, such as the nation, that teaches them as essential. A person with conventional values affirms those values and tries to express them in his or her life even if he or she does not always understand them. People affirm conventional values in order to give allegiance and support to the social structure that proclaims them. Questioning them, or choosing to affirm some and reject others implies a weakening of loyalty or faith in the church, nation, or other fundamental social system to which allegiance has been given. Therefore, the person with conventional values holds to them as a matter of faith, trusting that the wisdom inherent in them goes beyond his or her individual ability to understand.

Individuated values, at the opposite pole, are worked out by the individual. In contrast to conventional values, their referent is not the social system, but personal experience. The person with individuated values believes strongly that authentic values must come from personal decision, evolving out of increasing self-awareness and sensitivity to others. Just as the person with conventional values believes he or she betrays the group that teaches them by making individual decisions about them, so the person with individuated values believes that values taken on authority betray one's own authentic identity and lead to role-playing and self-deception. Carl Rogers, in *On Becoming a Person,* describes the process for individuated valuing: openness to experience, trust in one's organism as an instrument of sensitive living, internal focus of evaluation, and willingness to be a process.[4]

Life seems to consist of both conventional and individuated valuing. No one is able deliberately and consciously to invent values for the whole of life, and even if it were possible, the result would be barren and one-dimensional without the heritage of the race to draw upon. And on the other hand, no one can entirely abdicate personal decision making in modern society in those many areas where the authorities conflict or are silent or confused. The question is one of emphasis. The tension between conventional and individuated values is one of the most important conflicts in the Judaeo-Christian tradition as this tradition confronts contemporary social and cultural change.

As we have noted, conventional and individuated values are types, definitions of extremes of value systems that are not held in pure form by any actual human being. But they summarize the responses of persons in the study, and are based on their reports of their valuing processes. The following indicators were found to establish the degree of conventional or individuated valuing.

Milton Rokeach's list of eighteen so-called instrumental values was mentioned earlier. The respondents to our study were asked to rank the importance of each of these values in their own lives. The responses were subjected to factor analysis, the statistical treatment which attempts to identify a small number of underlying dimensions—in this case values—which can at least partially explain the rankings of the eighteen different values.

TABLE XII

Conventional vs. Individuated Values

POSITIVE		NEGATIVE	
obedient	.68	imaginative	−.71
polite	.58	intellectual	−.46
self-controlled	.53	courageous	−.36
clean	.40		

The positive side of this factor represents conventional values and the negative side, individuated values. The different religious traditions represented in our study differed significantly in their responses to this factor (statistically beyond .001.). Roman Catholics ranked highest on the conventional side, followed by conservative Protestants. Liberal Protestants were third, the "other" groups fourth, and Jews last. Since the words listed by Rokeach were not defined in the questionnaire and may have different meanings for different people, they should be regarded as only one set of indicators of conventional and individuated values. However, these words are used in the sermons and other teachings of churches and synagogues, and the factor analysis indicates (broadly, at least) the emphasis which members of the various religious groups place on conventional or individuated values.

Another indicator of the polarity of values is the rating system developed by Drs. O. J. Harvey and David Hunt to differentiate ways of processing information and making decisions. The system was developed to help teachers understand the reasoning process by which their students learn and apply new knowledge. We used the "This I Believe" instrument they developed in our study, adapting it slightly to our purposes.[5] Coders trained by Dr. Harvey were asked to rank the answers in terms of the following characteristics: their complexity or differentiation; their coherence or integration; the openness and candor expressed in the response; the number or quantity of evaluations, i.e., shoulds and oughts; the degree of normativeness, or definitions and rules; and the richness of language used. When the ratings on these seven characteristics were factor analyzed, they were found to fall into one major factor with high positive correlations for differentiation (.85), integration (.85), openness (.83), and candor (.76), and high negative correlations for evaluativeness ($-.72$), and normativeness ($-.71$). Persons ranking high on this Harvey-Hunt factor were considered to tend toward individuated values, and those ranking low to have conventional values. On this indicator the members of the various religious traditions in our study ranked much the same as on the previous factor. The "other" members had the most individuated values (.216), followed by liberal Protestants (.132) and Jews (.091). Conservative Protestants ranked fourth ($-.403$) and Roman Catholics last ($-.404$) on the measure of individuated values, and therefore highest on the conventional side. These differences were statistically significant beyond .001.

A number of measures pointed to this same polarity

between conventional and individuated values. Only one more will be mentioned, a factor indicating the kind of language persons used in responding to the "This I Believe" instrument. Responses were coded on the degree to which they contained explicitly religious language, symbols, and concepts rather than sociological, psychological, literary, popular cultural or other concepts and terms. Respondents were queried about their beliefs regarding twenty areas of life, including: God, the American Way of Life, guilt, prayer, time, Jesus, the purpose of life, race, doing good, conflict, institutions in our society, change, sin, people, sexual relationships, death, my career, myself.

This factor can also be considered an indicator of individuated values—relating the tradition of faith to the best of the new scientific and other secular thought of each age—as against conventional values—attempting to carry on the myth as if those developments had not happened. Groups that teach individuated values encourage their members to develop values mixed with secular concepts by the very process of incorporating secular thought in their teachings and applying the tradition to contemporary secular issues. Groups that hold conventional values attempt to isolate their teachings from these secular influences. On the conventional side of this factor, conservative Protestants ranked highest, followed by Roman Catholics. Liberal Protestants were third, with "others" fourth, and Jews last. Again, these differences are statistically significant beyond .001.

The distinction between conventional and individuated values is a distinction between two basically different ways in which religious groups are furnishing meaning-laden experiences to persons in contemporary society. Although very different, both are effective. There are effective and vital groups in our study at both ends of the spectrum as well as in the middle. Kelley's characteristics of strong groups (absolutism, conformity, discipline, commitment, missionary zeal, and fanaticism) pointed to the pole of conventional values.

THREE STYLES: THREE KINDS OF VITALITY

Groups that hold conventional values Kelley terms conservative, and holds that these are strong groups because they are growing in institutional strength (i.e., growing in membership and financial contributions) when compared to liberal churches. But we have seen that among the groups in our study, membership and financial giving are simply indicators of organizational activity, which is only one of three basic styles of participation in religious groups. Interpersonal relationships and personal religious experience and discipline, neither of which necessarily entail large membership and financial contributions, are also basic ways of expressing one's faith among the groups in this study.

There is a certain logic that connects conventional valuing with organizational activity as the primary behavioral response to faith. Belonging to the group itself, as the sole or primary source of values, is appropriately expressed in organizational activity; and the measure of one's loyalty to the faith is often understood as the amount of organizational activity engaged in. Since measures of organizational activity such as membership and financial giving are the most easily gathered data on organized religion, those groups in the Judaeo-Christian tradition which emphasize them are apt to be seen as more visible or "stronger" in relation to the rest of the tradition than they in fact are. But strong organizational activity in the religious institution itself is not a primary goal of many religious groups. Working for a better society, empowering the oppressed, living a life of love—for many religious bodies such aims are more important than building a strong organization.

It was suggested in the second chapter that with the loss of credibility of large organizations, Americans increasingly feel a need for authentic personal experience and close interpersonal relationships to restore meaning to their lives. In addition, competition between many meaning-making institutions to meet this need has meant that people's expectations have become more sophisticated. Some religious bodies meet the need for meaning by offering traditional values and encouraging traditional organizational activity. Some people gratefully accept such security, and these religious institutions, for example, conservative Protestant churches, prosper. Needs for interpersonal relationships and personal discipline may be powerfully met in the bargain. But many other people in society have concluded that the traditional ways simply do not work for them. They have found that more individuated valuing is necessary. And they are looking for meaning-making institutions, religious or otherwise, that directly offer interpersonal intimacy and authentic personal experience rather than emphasizing organizational activity. One may object that those who value personal and interpersonal experience are "sociologically naive"; that churches and synagogues must always transmit their tradition by membership, financial contributions, seminary graduates, and traditional programs that appeal to the motivation of belonging rather than intimacy or personal experience. But the religions of the world have influenced their societies in many different ways. And so we now see religious communities evolving and experimenting in order to meet needs in more immediate and appropriate ways.

Instead of participating in organizational activity, one's religious expression may involve finding or forming a friendship group or a small number of close friends with whom one can share deeply and find mutual support and enrichment in daily living. This process is often a genu-

inely religious enterprise because the friendships reinforce
a comprehensive view of life, related to the Judaeo-Christian tradition, and furnish a community in which to express it. Yet such networks of friends are not easy to
identify, let alone survey, and they are often unrelated to
the religious institution or exist on its periphery, perhaps
in the form of an adult discussion group. The interpersonal relationship response to the Judaeo-Christian tradition, which stresses intimacy rather than belonging, values
the organization and its activities as a means to an end
rather than as an end in itself. This response may be
associated with either conventional or individuated valuing. There are no denominational statistics or social surveys to estimate its importance as a behavioral response to
the Judaeo-Christian tradition in contemporary culture,
but the groups nominated to our study point to its importance.

The third response to religion that our study identifies
is that of personal experience and discipline. Along with
the need to belong and to express intimacy is the need for
authentic personal religious experience. It is expressed
through such activities as meditation, daily prayer, bible
reading, or solitary walks in the woods, which again are
not recorded in denominational statistics or social surveys
but which are very important in determining the shape
and influence of religion in contemporary culture. In some
traditions, discipline is emphasized, as in the practice of
daily prayer or regular bible reading. When discipline is
emphasized, it is often related to conventional valuing.
But for some people private religious activity means the
seeking of depth experiences by such various means as
quiet times or informal reveries, personal growth workshops, yoga, or other spiritual disciplines. Such people
usually hold individuated values, and their private religious activities are often unrelated to or unnoticed by
churches and synagogues. For example a man may spend

his Sunday mornings in meditation or doing something intentionally for the benefit of others. He may not belong to a church, and so his activities will not be recorded in any denominational yearbook. Many nominal churchgoers find their real religion in reading the Daily Word each morning, in yoga or other Eastern disciplines, or in practices from the human potential movement, although their pastor, if he knew about it, might oppose these practices or dismiss them as irrelevant.

Conservative churches *are* growing, as Kelley demonstrates, because they offer conventional meaning-laden experience and ask for the response of organizational activity in return. But other groups are also having an important impact, although it is hard to prove this statistically because they offer *individuated* meaning-laden experiences in the context of communities built directly on interpersonal relationships and personal religious experience and discipline. Some of those groups have been identified in this study. Here are two examples of groups appealing to young adults, one in a conventional and one in an individuated way. Both offer an exciting mixture of organizational activity, interpersonal relationships, and inner experiences.

Lighthouse Ranch

Lighthouse Ranch is seven acres of land and several buildings on a wild green bluff two hundred feet above the Pacific Ocean at the northern edge of California, just south of the town of Eureka. In 1970, a group of young Christians moved to the land, and invited the Reverend James Durkin to lead them. The group set up a nonprofit corporation, began purchasing the property, and started a storefront evangelistic ministry in Eureka.

Ranch members refer to Reverend Durkin as the "Presbyter of the Lighthouse" and recount that he organized them according to biblical precedent. People were appointed to leadership roles in various areas of work as they demonstrated interest and ability. Equally important, they were involved in the well-structured life of the church in Eureka, with preaching and prayer services twice during the week and twice on Sunday. Bible study classes emerged spontaneously at the ranch as persons felt themselves called to teach their brothers and sisters.

The first "onslaught" of new people came in the spring of 1971, when fifty additional people moved into the space only a dozen had occupied during the winter. Over the summer fifty more joined the Lighthouse community. Under Reverend Durkin's teaching and leadership, the social organization was cohesive enough to absorb the growth. Old buildings on the property were refurbished and became a men's dorm, a women's dorm, a kitchen and dining hall, and a married couples' dorm. Bible classes increased, as did the witnessing to newcomers. Participation in the structured round of ejaculatory prayers, singing, witnessing together, common meals, shared work, and the church services was sustained. Many of those who came in the summer stayed on into the winter, and for every one who left, at least one more came.

January of 1972 was a particularly lean time at the ranch. Meals consisted of thin soup and little else. But the community was sustained by faith, and funds were received when the need was greatest. One of the chief sources of income continues to be furnishing emergency clean-up crews when a freight train is wrecked in the area. Lighthouse people evidently work faster and better than anyone else and are regularly called. Often they are able to bring some of the wreckage, such as old lumber, back with them to help expand the ranch. They have also developed a very attractive crafts shop in Eureka, which sells excellent quality leather goods and other products made on the ranch, each of which carries a greeting in Christ to the person who buys it from the brother or sister who crafted the article.

Lighthouse also produces the shopping news for the Eureka area. The reader is apt to find the affirmation "Jesus is the Lord!" unexpectedly next to the A & P ad. In addition, the commune produces baked goods, which it sells in town, and intends to open its own bakery.

Lighthouse has become known to other Christian communes

throughout northern California, and has helped organize ecumenical gatherings and celebrations for the entire area. The group also sends out missionaries to infiltrate and convert "heathen" communes in the area and has even sent missionaries as far as Alaska.

If the term "Jesus people" has any merit at all in describing communes like Lighthouse, it is because it focuses on the total identification of life and thought with Christ as Lord. From such rejoinders as "Praise God," or "Thank you, Jesus," offered as frequently as "O.K." is in secular society, to the continual and intentional reference to Bible verses in stating an opinion or coming to a decision, to singing gospel songs while eating, working, and traveling; daily life and thought and personal interaction and relationships are all built around Jesus and biblical doctrine with a remarkable degree of intentionality. But the pattern is not forced; the group is spontaneous, has fun, and does not take itself too seriously. Great emphasis is placed on the loving and joyful quality of relationships. In the group interview, one person witnessed in a quiet and moving way to his conversion as a result of seeing how much people in the commune loved each other. And indeed there is a gentle, happy, and considerate quality to conversation and group life that has a powerful effect on the newcomer.

Many people come to Jesus and to Lighthouse after serious drug use, family separation and stress, and often lengthy periods of drifting from place to place. At Lighthouse Ranch aimlessness is replaced by a consistent and detailed ordering of life with great emphasis on teaching.

Lighthouse currently has about 130 members, rather evenly divided between men and women. There are several children, but ages range primarily from middle teens to late twenties, with a very small middle-aged group. Almost all are white. The socio-economic backgrounds are quite varied, but any indication of previous affluence or poverty is well submerged in the new communal life.

One of the main sources of teaching is the preaching of Reverend Durkin. His sermons are a complex exposition of human psychology of soul, mind, and body from Pauline sources interpreted in the evangelical tradition. The drama of his sermons is not in the color of language nor the fervor of delivery, but in the intrinsic chain of reasoning as it unfolds. To the observer this reasoning appears to be remarkably focused on the needs of young people for ego identity, clear direction, and stable structures for their lives. Doctoral candidates and university graduates who attend the sermons indicate that Reverend Durkin's teaching of biblical doctrine made good, as well as saving, sense to them.

Lighthouse members are living out of a total and unified vision of God, man, and the world. One of our questions asked participants to identify their own priorities for change out of forty cards listing various concerns. At the end of the group interview, one of the members recounted his evolution from Kennedy supporter to Berkeley street radical to Christian, and then, picking up the cards, scornfully stated that none of these problems would ever be solved piecemeal. God's kingdom was the single and total solution, and Christians could participate in it now.

Members' biblical faith and practice has led them to a style of life that is ecologically most advanced. The men sleep in a neat and well-organized dwelling in which each one's bed and private living space occupies a space approximately 3½ feet by 4 feet by 3½ feet. Their demands for food, clothing, and consumer goods are correspondingly modest. And they live this way not out of a sense of deprivation, but out of a joyous sense of being now in God's kingdom, to which every human will eventually come.

The group articulated its twofold purpose as to "preach the gospel and grow in grace." Preaching the gospel, of course, means much more than verbal pronouncements; it includes the total expression of the vision. Specific goals for the future include the expansion of the printing ministry and the development of an FM radio station, establishing a bakery and selling the products door-to-door, sending people out to new ministries overseas, an expanded in-town ministry, a "halfway house of helps" for those persons too "strung out" from their worldly state to benefit from life in the commune, reaching out to other ministries in fellowship, and beginning a school for children. Given their past accomplishments, one should not judge these hopes to be unrealistic. Lighthouse members believe that "in everything, God gives the plans and shows the group how to carry them out." The believers' duties are not to make long-term plans, but "to deny oneself and to live the Word in fellowship with God and each other twenty-four hours a day."

The total vision does become restrictive for some, and people talk about leaving Lighthouse for a time and then returning. There is also little tolerance for "dead" churches and those who do not preach the gospel "clearly and correctly." But the total vision, in personal lifestyle and relationships, social organization, economic sustenance, and relation to the rest of the world, is a consistent whole which has intriguing connections with issues such as ecology, justice, and liberation.

New Community Projects, Inc.

New Community Projects in Boston is the newest and perhaps most intriguing development of Interseminarian Incorporated. *Project Place,* the first of Interseminarian's programs, was begun in 1967 by Peter Calloway, a student at Harvard Divinity School, to minister to runaways and young people with drug and other personal problems in Boston. *Place* provided overnight lodgings, a switchboard for telephone counseling, and drop-in problem-solving counseling services. All three facets of the program grew rapidly until now sixty to eighty youngsters stay from one to fifteen days at *Place House* each month. About two-thirds are reconciled with their parents, the rest are referred for foster placements. *Place Switchboard* handles an astounding 30,000 calls a year.

In addition to Project Place, Interseminarian has more recently developed *Reach,* which extends the emergency hotline to the Boston metropolitan area, and offers a variety of drug education and training programs, including self-help peer group counseling programs, in schools and communities for youngsters, parents, and professionals.

The significance of Interseminarian and Place does not lie in these statistics of rapid growth. Fundamentally, Interseminarian is a distinctive and successful attempt to build a complex social service organization around countercultural values and aims. Its genesis was in the students' boredom with professional theological education and their search for ways to meet genuine human needs. They believe that these needs arise from the gap between rapid technological change and lagging cultural change. In the words of one of Interseminarian's proposals, "[This] is a world which is increasingly marked by transience, temporary organizations and systems, frequent changes in career, and loyalty to cooperative groupings rather than to a race, an institution, a profession, or a career. It is no wonder that people of the post–World War II generation (and older) find it difficult to relate to an ethos of individualism, static institutional loyalties, competitiveness, wars, and the solitariness of domestic life. Place intended to be literally and symbolically a place, congruent with the perceptions of young people about their world . . . which would help them to learn to cope with it, and which would help them mesh with older styles of life."

This goal meant that the group would have to be authentically countercultural in all its aspects, not only to fit members' own needs and perceptions of reality, but also to be congruent with the perceptions of those they wished to serve. The founders and members of Project Place felt bored and alienated from existing structures and discovered themselves able to help teenagers in personal distress from the same alienation. But the group then took the more difficult step of evolving an organizational form which fit their own intuitions and developing values, and which was also able to survive in the larger world.

The organization which evolved has several distinguishing characteristics. To use their own words, the "hierarchical pyramid is a shallow curve . . ." Repetitious or dull work is shifted from person to person so no one has to work more than half-time at it. While there are certainly leaders in the organization, "experienced persons tend to move 'horizontally' rather than 'up the ladder.' . . . Entry-level jobs include a high level of decision-making responsibility." Decision making and communications are handled by administrative committees made up of elected representatives of various programs and community meetings. The salary scale is also nonhierarchical and needs-

based. *All* staff receive the same basic salary—$5,000 per year
—which is adjusted only on the basis of need, such as providing
for children. The salary is intended to be adequate for a noncon-
sumerist lifestyle. "The philosophy behind our salary scale is
that society is wastefully overconsumptive and must learn to
share its productivity with the world's poor as well as with the
malnourished public sector. Besides, Interseminarian needs to
be highly cost-effective with limited resources. . . . Place will
provide $750,000 of services for $250,000 *and* keep and add to
its excellent staff."

Another interesting characteristic of Interseminarian is the
impressive list of medical, legal, financial, and other consultants
and part-time or volunteer help. These resources help maintain
the quality of Interseminarian's programs and establish its credibility with other institutions. Interseminarian relies on the community as an ally. Yet, it also maintains that professionals
categorize problems, while the staff and volunteers have to deal
with whole persons in whole life situations. The relationship
with professionals typifies the stance toward established institutions and values generally. The Interseminarian group intends
to form around its own countercultural values, but it also intends to survive in the "straight" world according to the criteria
of that world, i.e., growth, financial success, professional credibility.

A final important characteristic of the group is its refusal to
separate life into personal and professional spheres. The community has a farm in New Hampshire to which it travels once
a month during the winter for "community day"—actually a
weekend of celebration together.

Many staff live in communes, which was the genesis of New
Community Projects. In 1969 the staff of Interseminarian Incorporated leased a house so that they could live together and share
expenses. The experience was nourishing and positive, so the
next summer and fall three more houses were leased. No more
than half the residents of these houses were related to Project
Place. Three additional houses joined tangentially in a sort of
"group of groups," each group with its own characteristics and
experiences. Since the first house found not only that group
living was helpful for them but that they were able to be helpful

to other beginning groups, they began writing group histories to document their experience and teach others what they had learned.

In March, 1971, a community meeting at Interseminarian began New Community Projects, a counseling and consulting service for persons interested in joining communes and for communes themselves. Rick Paine, an ordained minister who had been one of the early members of Project Place, became the director. New Community Projects put an ad in the Boston underground paper and received sixty to eighty phone calls a week. The staff decided to work only with persons interested enough to take the further step of coming to a weekly meeting on communal issues. In May, the project began offering services to Beansprout, an informal association of forty communes in the Boston area. Both full-time and volunteer staff were added until there were four full-time and one part-time staff, and a number of volunteers. The competition for the few paid staff positions is considerable. In the fall of 1971, the Alternative Family Group was started to offer counseling and consulting to older adults with children who are interested in communal living.

New Community Projects is a most thoughtful and well organized attempt to deal directly with the increasing interest in alternative forms of intimate community and extended family life.

Religion of experience can be expressed through either conventional or individuated values. Either pole can be a vehicle for the interpersonal intimacy and religious experience and disciplines that express religion of experience. But what about the religious groups in the middle? In the Christian tradition, they are usually called the liberal churches—communities which try to hold together fidelity to the tradition and relevance to contemporary culture. Is religion of experience possible for these groups also? In the next chapter we will look at the findings from the study that bear on that question.

7

The Challenge to the Liberal Churches

One of the motivations for the Insearch study was to address the malaise of what are usually called the "main-line Protestant denominations" or the "liberal churches." These are the churches that had flourished after the Second World War, along with other religious bodies, responding to what Winters called the social interdependence and communal isolation of Americans.[1] Although they grew rapidly, these churches did not always accept that growth uncritically as a sign of God's favor.

Some of the more critical theologians tried to understand the phenomenon of growth in terms of the fullest claims of the Christian gospel. Colin Williams and others created a set of criteria of fidelity for the local church in *The Missionary Structure of the Congregation.*[2] And there were harsher critiques of the Church from within. From *The Suburban Captivity of the Church*[3] TO *The Comfortable Pew*[4] the Church engaged in a spate of self-criticism that had an almost ludicrous dimension—the way to guarantee book sales to the church market was to be harshly critical of the intended readers.

At best, the criticism was an attempt to keep the Church faithful to the fullest understanding of the message it proclaimed. But the postwar church carried out its mission in the midst of a time in human history when people experienced more change than continuity.

It is not a simple task to keep an institution faithful to a normative message in a changing culture and social order. Are we being obscurantist by insisting on a traditional formulation of the gospel in the face of new discoveries about the use of language? Have we lost our distinctive message by championing every new academic discovery and fashion in the popular culture? The liberal churches kept raising questions like these in a time of change, insisting that both a simple adherence to the faith in the form once and for all delivered to the saints and an uncritical enthusiasm for all new developments were equally false responses to the gospel.

The liberal churches raised these questions even when they threatened the power and self-interest of the questioners and the questioned. Reinhold Niebuhr and many others left us the permanent and painful insight that one's beliefs and values—and consequently, one's actions—are always at least partly determined by what enhances one's own political, economic, and psychic power. And yet despite, or perhaps because of, that insight, the ecumenical movement asked denominations to act against their self-interest and work toward a realization of Jesus' prayer that all may be one. Even more dramatically, churches involved in the civil rights movement asked millions of white Americans to act against their perceived self-interest and admit nonwhites to equal competition in politics and in the job and housing markets; and to sacrifice some of their own status and income to help minorities gain equal opportunities in education, self-esteem, and cultural advantages.

And so the liberal churches proceeded from the fifties through the sixties and into the seventies, raising the difficult issue of the relevance of the past to the present and the painful question of the place of power and self-interest in fulfilling the social claims of the gospel. Until this decade the churches could do all this and still be institutionally successful. Membership continued to grow faster than the population, and income grew fast enough that new mission claims did not threaten institutional survival. People kept coming to church, and ministries to blacks in Mississippi could be developed without the churches having to lay off the white executives who administered the funds. But in the seventies, statistics indicate that this happy situation no longer exists. Declining membership and income have fostered a sense of discouragement or even despair as church attendance decreases, national bureaucracies cut staff, and clergy have difficulty finding jobs.

THE DIFFUSION OF LIBERAL PROTESTANTISM

Several commentators have suggested that the reason the liberal Protestant churches are suffering so in the seventies is because of their commitment to relating the faith to the social issues of contemporary life. This commitment sometimes challenges the beliefs and arouses the resistance of parishioners who do not share their ministers' passions for social action. In *Gathering Storm in the Churches,* Jeffrey Hadden examined theological currents of the 1960s, especially among clergy, that led to a critique of national values and public policy.

The clergyman's new theology has moved him beyond the four walls of the church and prompted him to express God's love in concern for the world, particularly the underprivileged, and in the desire to change the structures of society. . . . The layman . . . seeks comfort and escape from the world in the sanctuary of God.[5]

Hadden felt that clergy stressed social issues partly because of their doubt or rejection of traditional doctrine. This doubt shifted the clergy's emphasis to a deeper concern about the meaning and implications of Christian faith for this world. In contrast, laity have maintained a loyalty to the church, but "it is questionable whether they maintain a high level of commitment. Religion has become privatized. Laity are more likely to say that what a man believes about religion is more important than what the church teaches. This privatization has stripped the church and clergy of much authority."[6]

As a result, in contemporary Protestantism, "there is no consensus as to what is believed, as to what is central and what is peripheral, nor is there any clear authority to resolve the uncertainty."[7] People are no longer sure what they believe and how the churches fit into their lives.

Thus, Hadden concludes: "As doubt about the validity of Christian belief emerges, commitment to actual participation in religious institutions declines. In other words, with doubt comes a rejection of the church's authority to demand regular participation in the life of the church."[8]

If this analysis is correct, we should expect to find a lack of consensus and uncertainty or confusion of belief even among the liberal Protestant groups in our study, which were picked as being especially vital. Disagreements about belief and authority, confusion about norms for church participation should be present if Hadden's analysis is correct. In fact, that is exactly what we found among the liberal Protestant groups in our study.

Using a technique called "discriminate analysis," we distinguished the Roman Catholic, conservative Protestant, liberal Protestant, Jewish, and non-Judaeo-Christian groups from each other in terms of their beliefs and characteristics of their community life. Discriminate analysis is a way to compare the beliefs and characteristics of each person in the study with the beliefs and characteristics of all other participants grouped by theological tradition. Thus, person A, who is a liberal Protestant, is compared with all Catholics, conservative Protestants, liberal Protestants, Jews, and others, to ascertain whether he is more like other liberal Protestants or more like members of other religious groups.

Roman Catholics were found to be distinguished from other groups in several ways: preference for explicitly religious language, the importance of interpersonal relationships in the group, and their lack of concern for social or personal change.

Conservative Protestants ranked even higher in their preference for using explicitly religious language, had many personal change concerns, and rated the importance of belonging to and participating in church very high. Conservative Protestants were less involved in other voluntary associations, and had fewer social and political concerns and activities than other groups. Jewish groups were distinctive in a number of ways: the high importance attached to belonging to the synagogue, the high level of social concern, their low use of explicitly religious language, low number of personal change concerns, and low commitment to personal religious disciplines. Even the groups in the "other" category, grouped only by their lack of an explicit Christian or Jewish identity, had in common a high level of concern for personal change, political activism, and social change. They could also be distinguished by their lack of use of explicitly religious language.

Liberal Protestants in the study, however, differ so much from each other they seemed to have very little in common overall except a low interest in personal religious discipline. It needs to be pointed out that this category has more groups in it than the others, and includes black and white groups. Nevertheless, the analysis seems to support the conclusion that liberal Protestants are most caught in the midst of cultural confusion and least able to find clear direction and identity through their religious affiliation.

This diffuseness of the liberal Protestants compared to the other major categories of groups in the study is demonstrated strikingly in the following table. In this table, each person in the study is placed in the category his or her beliefs most resemble as shown by the discriminate analysis. Thus, if a person in a Catholic group is more like most conservative Protestants in his valuing than like his fellow Catholics, he or she is placed in the conservative Protestant column in the row of Catholics. If the person most resembles other Catholics, he or she is placed in the Catholic column in the Catholic row. The response of liberal Protestants in the sample indicates a diffusion of belief and a diversity of valuing pattern greater than any other group. Liberal Protestants "lost" members to "Other," Jewish and Roman Catholic valuing categories—to every group except the conservative Protestants. Roman Catholics, Conservative Protestants, and Jewish respondents tended to identify more closely with their group profile.

This data raises important questions. Why is there such diffusion and lack of group identity among liberal Protestants? Has liberal Protestantism been doing something wrong? Is the liberal vocation of relating the past to the present and the imperatives of faith to the social order somehow self-defeating? Based on the experiences of the groups in our study, we think not. We do believe, however, that liberal churches have neglected personal religious experience and discipline. And we believe that this neglect of an essential aspect of faith has contributed to the institutional distress and self-doubt of the liberal churches. The groups in the Insearch study have something significant to say about each of these three aspects of the vocation of the liberal churches: relating the past to the present, the social imperatives of the gospel, and personal religious experience.

TABLE XIII

Coherence of Group Categories According to Valuing Patterns of Their Members

VALUING PATTERN

GROUP CATEGORY PARTICIPANT IS ACTUALLY MEMBER OF	ROMAN CATHOLIC	CONSERVATIVE PROTESTANT	LIBERAL PROTESTANT	JEWISH	OTHER	TOTAL
Roman Catholic	34	6	3	4	4	51
Conserv. Protestant	6	19	4	1	3	33
Liberal Protestant	17	9	43	22	29	120
Jewish	2	1	5	37	4	49
Other	3	1	17	4	38	63
Total	62	36	72	68	78	316

RELATING THE PAST TO THE PRESENT

The liberal churches place themselves in the middle of the continuum between conventional and individuated valuing. On the one hand, they depend upon tradition and therefore teach conventional values, and on the other hand, they are committed to translating and adapting their heritage according to the increasingly rapid changes of modern culture and thought. The consequence seems to be diffusion of identity and image, and confusion about how to renew vision while being faithful to tradition. The analyses of Hadden and others and the data from our study indicate that the liberal Protestant groups were more lacking in clarity of identity than the other theological traditions. In a time of continuing change, it probably cannot be otherwise.

The problem for the liberal churches is how the tradition ought to relate to contemporary culture. Scientific findings and cultural change continually reshape our understanding of human life. Those parts of the Judaeo-Christian tradition which deal with areas of experience denied by current scientific and cultural myths may be neglected or forgotten. And churches and synagogues may find themselves fighting over obsolete issues, overlooking that part of their message that relates to a new cultural concern. There is no guaranteed way to know which institutional form or specific belief is necessary to the integrity of the Judaeo-Christian message and which is the artifact of another culture that may be safely discarded when relating the myth to contemporary life. In the continuing contest of myths the lines will constantly shift while the attempt is made to present the full message or gospel in relation to changing cultural concerns and new scientific and philosophical knowledge. But revelation is necessary to counter-balance the advance of science as the sole source of new knowledge. The Judaeo-Christian tradition, is not our invention. Like common law, it has accrued through the ages from those who were changed by their relationship to God, and there is wisdom in it beyond what we can explain at any one point in the history of the development of scientific knowledge. In the process of relating the tradition to contemporary thought and life we may discover some part of that wisdom afresh from time to time.

Being in the middle between conventional and individuated valuing can be an opportunity and a source of strength. And it can be exciting. Churches such as Glide, St. Francis Presbyterian, COACT, and others in this study show the vitality of an honest and open encounter between faith and life.

THE SOCIAL IMPERATIVES OF THE GOSPEL

Hadden and many others documented the struggles of the liberal churches in the 1960s trying to be faithful to the social imperatives of faith. The 1970s brought even more resistance to the social gospel aspect of the liberal vocation. In June, 1972, Potomac Associates and the Gallup Organization cooperated in carrying out a national survey of Americans, published under the title, *State of the Nation.*[9] A comprehensive series of questions was asked about various aspects of American life, including twelve domestic areas, six international areas, and questions about government and the quality of life. Two main findings summarize the responses. The first is a lack of confidence in the quality of the national life. The second finding is that Americans are drawing back from the social commitments of the 1960s into private and personal concerns and preoccupations. Let us look at each of these findings briefly.

The *State of the Nation* survey found that with significant exceptions, Americans generally feel they are doing well in their personal lives, but there is considerable uneasiness among them about the conditions of national life. The Institute for Social Research of the University of Michigan reported in the spring of 1972 "a widespread feeling that the quality of life in this country has been deteriorating. Americans can give considerably more examples of ways that life in this country is getting worse than ways it is getting better."[10] A Harris poll released in June, 1972 reported that 68 percent of the public agreed with the statement, "The rich get richer and the poor get poorer," and 50 percent with "The people running the country don't really care what happens to people like yourself." While the public no longer thought the country had lost ground over the last five years (as it did in 1971, for the first time in the history of public opinion polls), the best that could be said was that America was now holding its own.[11]

Major institutions, and especially government, have suffered a loss of credibility in this decade. A surprising 54 percent of Americans believe that "a basic change will need to be made in the way our governmental system is now set up and organized."[12] Since 1972, of course, the incredible series of lies, deceptions, and admitted and alleged criminal acts by a president of the United States and his personal staff has been revealed. It is reasonable to believe, therefore, that dissatisfaction with government and the felt need to change it has grown considerably since 1972.

But the response of Americans to social crisis and loss of credibility in major institutions in the early 1970s has not been an increased commitment to social change. Indeed, quite the opposite. *State of the Nation* documents in a number of ways the increasing social apathy and introspection of Americans. The turn from public social concerns to private personal concerns is evident in attitudes toward a number of domestic and international problems.

Overall, the results of the survey show that "even when the context was explicitly national, the horizons of the people in viewing their country's situation were distinctly limited. Unless prodded by interviewers, only small minorities of Americans in mid-1972 seemed preoccupied with most of the major problems that confronted the nation. Significantly, our survey failed to uncover any topic of intensely concentrated concern among Americans, with the possible exception of the war/peace theme."[13]

Religious institutions have a responsibility to counter the apathy and disillusionment with public life. There is great temptation, and many seem quite unable to resist it, to simply draw back from social commitments and pander to privatized religion. But the agony of the churches and synagogues in the social struggles of the 1960s was the agony of America. A faithful congregation should not expect to prosper while those it is called to serve suffer. And many religious institutions did attempt to give up their organizational security and even existence for the sake of the world in the last decade. Any assessment of their effectiveness depends on how much social impact one can expect from voluntary organizations such as churches, which are marginal indeed in the power structure of America. But it may turn out that one of the churches' and synagogues' better hours for America, viewed from the long perspective of history, was their participation in the civil rights movement and the resistance to the war in Southeast Asia, and their attempts to sensitize their own membership to the need for empowerment of oppressed peoples. The fundamental social issues have not disappeared, nor have they been resolved, and faithful witness is still demanded by the God of love. Religious institutions must continue to be willing to pay the costs of faithful witness by disregarding organizational security.

America is the richest and most technologically advanced nation in a world where most nations are pressing for a more equitable share of wealth. White Americans have benefited from the genocide of the Native Americans, and the enslavement and exploitation of black and brown peoples. And none of these groups has yet achieved equality with whites by any socio-economic indicator. White middle-class Americans have perpetuated a culture of poverty in the midst of affluence. White male middle-class Americans have benefited from the inferior status of women in the family and the workplace. These inequalities persist, and any attempt to buttress them by means of the Christian tradition is a perversion of that tradition. The tradition calls instead for a redefinition of self-interest and of the kind of power needed to fulfill that self-interest. The challenge is to believers who have the power to fulfill more narrowly defined self-interests at the ultimate expense of others. Will those believers relinquish some of that power to the powerless, as their tradition demands?

The recent disclosures of corruption and immorality in Washington present a challenge to the social dimensions of faith. We need a ministry to cope with the apathy and disillusionment with government and with the quality of national life. The strength of the religious tradition must witness to the strength of the national myth, that we may have the courage to cleanse and reform our national life. As Americans Christians and Jews hunger for meaning-laden experiences that will allow them to believe again in the contribution America can make to the peace and justice of the world.

There is, and has to be, a national myth. Democracy will not survive without it. Our system of government is not simply a utilitarian arrangement, but is based on standards of how human beings ought to live together and on commitments to the common good. When these underlying values erode and are not renewed by fresh vision, democracy is subverted by private gain and tyranny threatens. Religious institutions have the delicate task of carrying out a lover's quarrel with political life, supporting its basic values while criticizing its injustices and pressing for reform.

PERSONAL RELIGIOUS EXPERIENCE

The most neglected aspect of the liberal vocation is nurturing personal religious experience. Even among the groups in our study, the only characteristic in which liberal Protestants were distinctive in the discriminate analysis was their lack of interest in personal religious experience. This lack of interest comes at a time when interest in informal experiential religion is bursting out all over. Liberal Protestants seem to have been taught to ignore that aspect of the faith which is most alive in the culture—personal religious experience—and their church life has suffered as a result. There are clear historic reasons for this neglect.

The fundamental principle of the liberal vocation is to relate the tradition to the best of contemporary thought. Until very recently, contemporary secular thought has been singularly ill-equipped to deal with the need for personal religious experience. Some psychologies have simply ignored this area of inner life. They have regarded inner reality as a black box about which nothing needed to be known in order to understand human behavior. Only the behavior inputs and outputs needed to be studied; the black box was merely the inferred link between the two. Such an approach certainly leaves the field of religious experience open to the theologians, but it also devalues this experience as inconsequential to the understanding of human beings.

The important revolution in psychology wrought by Freud legitimated the serious investigation not only of the contents of the psyche, but of those contents of which the person himself or herself was not even conscious. However, Freud did not count experiences described as "the presence of God" to be phenomena worthy of study in their own right. Since Freud was a doctor, his psychological discoveries were means to the end of curing his patients of specific disabilities. He did notice that religious beliefs and activities were often associated with the ailments he was treating. But his own view was that such beliefs and activities were usually symptoms of obsessive-compulsive neurosis. He regarded religion as the archaic projection of primitive people attempting to survive in a dangerous world by believing in a powerful helper. In a scientific age, humans would replace religion with the scientific method as the only effective means of understanding and mastering reality.

The psychology of religion grew up painfully trying to apply these pioneering psychological efforts to the experience of God, particularly as that experience occurred in the Judaeo-Christian tradition. But it foundered against the Freudian assumption that religious experiences and activities were primarily symptoms of mental disorder. The nadir of the effort was James Leuba's work in 1912, reducing the experiences of Christian mystics to the symptoms of hysteria.[14] On the other hand, the most important contribution of the early psychologists was the clinical study of ways in which religion did indeed contribute to mental illness, and the development of a method to treat people troubled by rigid and tyrannical religious beliefs.[15]

Treating the psyche as either a black box or a region of mental illness precluded valuing the experience of God's presence as the highest human goal. Early psychology had dehumanized and depersonalized the inner life. What place was there for faith and moral virtue, that is, for exercise of the will if personal difficulties were merely symptoms of unconscious conflict beyond the reach of will, curable only by medical treatment? The presence of God would be at best a misleading metaphor, since the only center of initiative in the psyche was the conscious ego attempting to control primitive impulses and internalized prohibitions. So theologians who wished to relate the religious tradition to contemporary thought had to turn their attention away from religious experience, and essential aspects of their tradition were badly neglected.

No metaphor which denied so much human experience could go unchallenged, and psychology today is not where it was when Leuba's book appeared. Specifically, there are a wide variety of metaphors guiding contemporary psychological inquiry in its attempt to study a broader range of human experience. The existentialist philosophers, existentialist psychotherapists, and ego psychologists brought will and decision making back into the psyche, and existentialist theologians appropriated their work. Back in the 1930s Anton Boisen anticipated them when he found that his struggle with schizophrenia was a test of his will. His study of other schizophrenic episodes convinced him that psychosis is often a struggle for self-definition in which personal courage and choice are essential to recovery.[16] R. D. Laing currently maintains the same outlook, perceiving full dimensions of personhood, including conscious choice and the search for meaning, in the experience of the "mentally ill."[17]

Humanistic psychologists have been insisting for some time now that human potential as well as human illness should be studied, and that our knowledge of the psyche is skewed because too much of it is based on investigations of "sick," instead of "healthy" people. "Growth," "self-actualization," and "human potential" are metaphors that helpfully redirect our attention to essential aspects of personhood overlooked by the mental illness model.

Religious experience is now considered by some a phenomenon worthy of study in its own right. Abraham Maslow, who did pioneering work in the field of inner experience, began by interviewing people who, more than most of us, were gifted and were fulfilling their life's promise. He discovered that certain experiences were common to these "self-actualizing" persons. He called these "peak experiences," i.e., experiences of the essential unity of reality, deriving from a sense of connectedness with all life in which each person or thing is enjoyed and cherished for its own sake. The person with peak experiences feels simultaneously very humble and very powerful, open to reality and not personally threatened by it. Maslow's reports of peak experiences sound very like the reports of mystical experiences in the Judaeo-Christian and other great religious traditions. Maslow came to believe that self-actualizing persons are truly characterized by this ability to have peak or transcendent experiences. During the last part of his life he reported that the transcendent experiences themselves had become less important for him than the residue they left behind—a certain attitude toward life. He called this attitude "unitive consciousness," for it integrated an awareness and sensitivity to all the pain and suffering in life *sub specie aeternitas* with an overarching experience of the unity and goodness of life and one's place in it. Maslow kept proposing that these experiences be studied seriously like any other psychological phenomena.[18]

Although there seems to be, as yet, little theological interest in such work, many psychologists have taken up the challenge. The *Journal of Transpersonal Psychology* reports some of their work, which ranges widely over theoretical issues and practical research.[19] But what is most impressive about the best of these researchers is their sensitivity to the enormous value questions raised by their work. Many of them seem to realize that such research must involve their own pilgrimage to spiritual growth and maturity. These psychological researchers are greatly interested in the disciplines and beliefs of the major religions as sources of insight in their work. Also, they recognize the danger that "altered states of consciousness" may be marketed and the hunger for them exploited for trivial or destructive purposes.

Serious work is going forward, basically out of touch with the Judaeo-Christian tradition. I participated in a seminar of transpersonal psychologists in which those present spoke movingly of the basic human and philosophical questions raised in their work, and of their personal search for religious beliefs and disciplines to address those questions. The psychologists had found help in such religious disciplines as Sufism, Yoga, and Buddhism, and had learned from contemporary disciplines such as Psychosynthesis. But I was the only person present who had found the Judaeo-Christian tradition to be his major guide and source of insight. These psychologists are working on the frontiers where science and religion meet, and they find themselves drawing insight from traditions where psychology and spiritual growth have been seen as one for millenia. Meanwhile, most theologians who are concerned about these matters still struggle to accommodate a secular psychology with little room for religious concerns. Their efforts are badly out of date. As a result, Jews and Christians are often cut off even from the spiritual disciplines of their own tradition, because there is no way to think about them or practice them in contemporary terms. Consequently, some theologians are still preoccupied with helping people in a secular world *talk* about the experience of God while some psychologists are actively helping people *experience* the presence of God.

These developments are a challenge to, and an opportunity for, liberal Protestants to practice their vocation of relating religious tradition to contemporary thought in an area where people hunger for experience. Liberal Protestants often seem to fear that such efforts would be a "new pietism" in which authentic personal experience would undercut social commitments. The groups in our study did not seem to experience such difficulties. COACT, Glide, and St. Francis Presbyterian all seem to successfully combine personal religion and social commitments.

8

On Doing Something About It

We started with a hunch: that response to the cultural hunger for experience represents the growing edge of religion in America. We looked at some reasons why there is a hunger for experience in contemporary culture and why religion in America has historically been primarily a religion of experience. Then we tested our hunch by asking a large panel of church and synagogue leaders to nominate what they considered to be promising and vital religious communities that might offer some insights about the future of religion in this culture. We organized their suggestions into categories, and selected examples from each category for intensive study. We did not study a representative sample of American religious life, but a representative sample of the religious groups that a large number of well-informed religious leaders considered to be vital and suggestive of the growing edge of American religion. You have read brief descriptions of the groups and longer case studies of some of them. You have seen that the members of these groups tend to be unusually well-informed and active in religious organizations, that their religious experiences tend not to be associated with formal worship, and that they are groping for new religious language to express what they experience. They re-

133

gard loving as the highest value, and are unusually concerned about their own personal growth, development, and security. They are critical of American society, but optimistic about changing it, and often involved in specific social change activities. In fact, they are generally more optimistic than Americans about life and the influence of religion.

We also found some important themes within the groups themselves that cut across theological and organizational categories. Each group seems to specialize in one or another of several fundamental concerns. Some groups emphasize the grounding of social concerns in intentional, continually re-thought theological presuppositions. Other groups grow through a fresh presentation of traditional beliefs and organizational forms. A third set of groups emphasizes walking in the ways of the Lord in all aspects of one's personal life. A fourth cluster specializes in social action from a more humanitarian or pragmatic base, less explicitly tied to theological intentions. A fifth major concern is the personal growth or happiness of the individual, and the group exists only to foster that growth. And a final set of groups exists to realize alternative lifestyles from a more or less explicitly countercultural model. The study also identified three basic styles of participation in these groups: organizational activity, interpersonal intimacy, and personal religious experience and discipline. We noted, too, that behind a strong group there is usually a strong charismatic leader. Finally, we discovered that the liberal Protestant groups in our study share the confusion and diffusion of beliefs that have been reported generally for this tradition.

But what of the future? What place is there for the church or synagogue in the future of religion in America?

Churches and synagogues are not the only institutions helping people to achieve their humanity. And whether churches and synagogues grow or decline in the years ahead depends partly on their ability to furnish meaning-laden experiences to those who hunger for them. People need new or renewing experiences that connect the various areas of their lives and give them meaning. Secular meaning-making institutions are becoming ever more sophisticated in offering such experiences, and churches and synagogues are in competition with them. Communities in the Judaeo-Christian tradition define their fundamental differences in a variety of ways: some by beliefs or by evidences of sanctity, others by liturgy, ethnic background, or by participation in a mystical community. But today they share a common characteristic: many people come to them to find meaning-laden experiences that will put the rest of their lives together. The vitality of their faith and community life will depend in part on the extent to which they recognize and address this need. For this hungering for experiences is simply the contemporary way in which people are seeking the knowledge of the love of God.

In the beginning of this book we said that religion of experience is not unambiguous. The emotional power of it can deepen one's prejudices and self-righteousness. It can, and has at times, become elitist, putting burdens of guilt and inadequacy on those who cannot achieve certain states of consciousness. And it can appeal to and support privatism and social irresponsibility in American religion. Theologians have the task of helping to set the norms for religion of experience. Which experiences, powerful and meaningful though they may be, are faithful to, and which are denials of, the God of love? Such theological work is much needed, and scholars like Harvey Cox and Martin Marty are turning their attention to the task.[1]

But people do not seek theological talk about how one can discuss the experience of God. They hunger for the actual *presence* of God. Theologians set norms for evaluating experience according to their intellectual understanding of the tradition. And the writings of great theologians like Paul Tillich can themselves furnish occasions for the experience of God. But one has to have experience before guides and judgments about experience make any sense. Theology has been rightly preoccupied with helping people understand religious tradition intellectually in the light of modern philosophy. But theologians have greatly neglected what they could have learned from their own historic faiths, or from Eastern religions, or even from transpersonal psychology: that theory is not an end in itself, but a means to more faithful practice. When I visited a Zen center recently, the talk was about the "practice." Zen Buddhism has a sophisticated and subtle intellectual tradition, but it exists for the sake of the practice, the meditation, the living. Theology should exist for the sake of experience, and should be judged by that experience as well as judging it. People today hunger for the experience of reality out of which life's meaning may come, not for *discussion* of reality.

Each community in the Judaeo-Christian tradition proclaims and attempts to live out its faith in the God of Love, who creates and redeems humankind and the cosmos itself. Each community passes on its heritage of culturally conditioned forms by which God was known in the past. And in each community fresh revelations of God, and a changing and conflicting culture conspire to make those past forms problematic. How does one sing the Lord's song in a strange land, increasingly strange because of the forces of change? In our study of a diversity of communities in the Judaeo-Christian tradition, we have identified two quite different general approaches to the problem. The first, practiced by some conservative Protestant, Roman Catholic, and Jewish groups in the study, has been to emphasize the continuity and security of traditional beliefs and community forms in a time of change. Such an approach provides one clear answer to the problem of living with the complexities of modern life. It especially appeals to people who have, or feel they have, little power to affect the conditions of their lives. This may include such diverse groups as blue collar workers threatened by competition in the job market, and over-privileged adolescents who have been denied the values and structures that would enable them to build a stable personal identity. In the act of teaching conventional valuing through organizational activity, such groups often provide personal religious discipline and experience, and close interpersonal relationships. Thus their effectiveness is augmented by providing occasions for experiences that give power and meaning to life. These groups may, as Lighthouse Ranch does, even anticipate complex ecological issues by adopting an egalitarian community life and reduced patterns of consumption. But if they do so, it is not because of preoccupation with forecasting the future, but because of their trust in and adherence to their traditional beliefs and structures.

The other general approach has been to accept and even celebrate the advance of science and technology and increasing pluralism, and to nurture personal growth and social change through the insights of behavioral science or by courting revolutionary ideologies. Groups taking this approach teach individuated valuing, encourage their members to develop personal identity and direction out of their own individual living, and use pluralistic symbols and beliefs in addition to the resources of the religious tradition. Sometimes this approach is basically intellectual in content; at other times it is an attempt to furnish meaning-laden experiences of interpersonal relationships and the presence of God. Groups taking these approaches may be in the mainstream, on the periphery, or even outside the major faiths of the Judaeo-Christian tradition. Sometimes, according to some data in our study, there is a diffuseness or lack of direction in such groups that makes it difficult for those looking for clear experience to find it there. In attempting to be relevant to every new social crisis and scientific idea, some groups actually lose the ability to be relevant, overlooking their obligation to furnish strong and understandable myths and community forms that give power and meaning to life.

Sometimes such groups show a decline in statistics of organizational activity because they have threatened the self-interest of their own members through their social activism. But, on the other hand, there is something unseemly and basically wrong about a church that is happy and thriving while the culture is in agony. The agony of churches and synagogues in the last decade has been part of the agony of America, and if they are to be faithful to their vocation, churches and synagogues must continue to struggle. They must continue to struggle because none of the great social crises of our time show any signs of going away. The task of taking charge of technology instead of letting it control our lives, and of relating the discoveries of science to the fundamental human issues of meaning is more urgent than ever. The problems of the cities will not go away. The emerging ecological crises may force suburbs into cooperation with cities if there is to be a livable environment for anyone, rich *or* poor. And no one seriously expects women, youth, blacks, and the poor to just give up their drive for empowerment and return to a former state.

The confusion regarding organizational activity needs to be resolved. It is not reasonable for religious groups to criticize their traditions' preoccupation with institutional statistics, and then to be disappointed when such indicators of maintenance as membership and finances begin to drop off. Theologians preach that the Church exists not to preserve itself but for the sake of the world, but administrators sophisticated in the social sciences know that to effect change in the world one must build an effective institution. There is no necessary contradiction between

these two insights. Organizations, and especially voluntary organizations, need to change form in a changing
culture. There is a great deal of thought and experimentation going on—some of it reported in this book—seeking
a variety of shapes for effective and faithful church organizations. Neither an unreasoning defense of the past nor a
faddish preoccupation with novelty is very helpful. What
is needed is continuing faithful and pragmatic devotion to
the task of hearing the Lord's voice in a strange land,
knowing that change is the only constant.

But the decline in institutional maintenance statistics is
indeed lamentable when it is due not to faithfulness to the
social implications of God's message, but to neglect of the
authentic interpersonal and religious experiences people
are seeking. Theologians' devotion to accommodating
modern thought has left the realm of religious experience
largely to the charismatics, unregarded groups of mystics,
followers of Eastern disciplines, and, ironically, humanistic psychologists, who are not so awed by the authority of
scientific paradigms. We have seen the group dynamics
movement, the clinical pastoral training movement, and
now the first religious fruits of the human potential movement all attempt to reintroduce experience in general, and
religious experience in particular, into the lives of the
communions that emphasize individuated valuing. Such
efforts are usually relegated to the "practical" (i.e., inferior) side of the seminary curriculum; too eagerly seized
upon by administrators as a gimmick to make churches
attractive; used as a substitute for theology by some; and
regarded with disdain by serious theologians and ethicists.
Too seldom are they regarded as signals from the secular
culture itself to recall churches and synagogues to their
true vocation of furnishing occasions for living in the presence of God. While theologians talk about how one can
talk about the experience of God, a motley assembly of
saints and charlatans in the culture has been experiment-

ing with a variety of paths to the experience itself. Our hope is that the faiths in the Judaeo-Christian tradition may reclaim that part of their own heritage that speaks to the contemporary cultural need for experience.

Appendix A

GROUPS THAT PARTICIPATED IN THE INSEARCH
STUDY

(see also chart, page 38)

THE ABBEY OF NEW CLAIRVAUX is a Trappist monastery in
Vina, California, which was begun with twenty-eight members
when the order decided to found a house on the West Coast in
1955. Currently there are twenty-five members in the community, ranging in age from 24 to 70, with the average age around
40. Some were professional men, others blue-collar workers,
soldiers, or college students before entering the monastery. One
monk is Chicano, the rest white. The community supports itself
on the income from a 586-acre farm in the Sacramento Valley,
growing prunes and English walnuts.

Trappists, formerly referred to as the "Marine Corps of the
Catholic Church," were challenged in the mid-sixties to find
ways of implementing *aggiornamento.* "We had to learn how to
interact with each other," said one monk. Each now recognizes
his responsibility for his own spiritual growth. No longer can a
monk simply depend on the rules of the community. The abbey,
however, remains cloistered, with monks rising every morning
at 3:15 to combine meditation, hard work on the farm, and
study throughout the day within a Benedictine liturgical framework. Union with God and community with one another are the

aims of the monastery, whose simple and straightforward orthodoxy guides all aspects of the monks' "life under the rule and under the abbot." (For fuller discussion, see Chapter 3.)

BRANDEIS CAMP INSTITUTE in southern California was created by Rabbi Shlomo Bardin in 1941 to communicate the Jewish experience to young people and adults. Brandeis Camp is a retreat center attended by hundreds of persons each year for weekends or longer. The entire environment is designed to be an experience in living the Jewish heritage. Insights and methods from the personal growth movement, including group process, sensitivity training, and art education are used to explore feelings as well as ideas. The goal is to discover or reaffirm one's own personal Jewish identity and out of that identity to find direction for living.

The staff and board are mostly middle-aged, and middle-class Jews who raise and administer a budget of slightly less than one-half million dollars a year to carry on the Institute's program.

THE CHICAGO CENTER FOR BLACK RELIGIOUS STUDIES was founded at the end of 1970 by twelve men in religion and the professions to fulfill three needs: (1) to make theological, biblical, and religious training available to the Black community, (2) to reverse the historic failure of white seminaries in recruiting a "significant black presence" and to provide a relevant, high quality education for blacks, (3) to meet the demands of the black revolutionary leadership for providing more relevant involvement of black churchmen in the struggles of Black people. Since that time, the Center has grown to ninety members, mostly young adults, and a budget somewhat under $100,000 a year. The Center offers courses in the community; staff members teach in Chicago seminaries; and the Center conducts "intensives" in which groups of twenty examine the Black situation from various perspectives—theological, educational, economic, etc. The Center has also involved itself in community activities, such as boycotts, organizing voter registration, Operation PUSH, and is developing a prison ministry.

COACT (Community of Active Christians Today) is a series of house churches in Waco, Texas, with no paid leadership, heavy involvement in personal growth and organization development training, and strong commitment to a variety of social change projects in the community. Founded with forty members in early 1970, COACT's sixty current members have been involved in a variety of human potential and human relations labs, and have formed small groups with lay leadership for sharing, study, and support. Temporary systems are important in COACT's organizational style—study groups and task forces form, work, and then disband rather than trying to achieve permanent existence. The congregation, which is white, cross-generational, and middle-class, has split into two, then three house churches. The entire program of the church runs on a budget of $8,000. Ken Solberg, the founding pastor and a Lutheran clergyman, has worked himself out of a job: the group decided that it could function without a professional leader, since leadership was so widely shared among lay people. Representative of COACT's involvement in twenty-four community service projects is its coalition with Project Self-Help, which aims at generating jobs, free breakfasts, financial assistance, and community organizing in the Black community. (For fuller discussion, see Chapter 4.)

THE CHURCH OF THE CELEBRATION, in San Dimas, California grew out of role-playing workshops led by Rev. Bob Blees on the invitation of the Southern California Yokefellows. Between the years of 1967 and 1969, a nucleus of forty to sixty persons formed who had participated in the workshops and wanted "a belonging part" of the program as well as a "becoming part." In 1969, an experimental ministry was begun under the aegis of the United Church of Christ, and it has since grown to a congregation of 350 members. Bob Blees and an associate contribute half their income from leading personal growth workshops toward the $60,000 annual budget of the congregation. Members supply around 20 percent of the church's income. The membership, which varies widely in age, class, religious background, and race (although predominantly white), joins the church through role-play workshops, which the ministers say are, like baptism, an initiatory rite. In the workshops persons experience acceptance, discover that it is all right to be who they are, and discover new ways of relating to and achieving intimacy with the group. The church program also includes two monthly celebrations (one led by ministers, the other by laity), quarterly "total involvement" live-in weekends, Bible study, rock concerts, poetry readings, personal sharing, and individual counseling of group members by the ministers. Lay people assume most organizational leadership. There are no creeds or beliefs as conditions for membership, and little that reminds one of church in the traditional sense. In their own words, the group's goal is "to be a community in which growth at your own pace and relationships are possible." "Growth" means self-acceptance, discovery of one's own freedom and creativity, and nurturing the growth of others. (For fuller discussion, see chapter 4.)

COMMIT is an independent, nonprofit corporation for training and consultation, founded in 1966 and located in Los Angeles, California. One of a number of action training agencies which came into existence all over the country in the mid-sixties, COMMIT has grown steadily in the range of its programs, its effectiveness, and its staff—six trainers, including two women, a black, and a Chicano. Its current budget is around $125,000. The director, Rev. Speed Leas, encourages the staff/members, characterized as "self-starters," to develop and implement their own contracts with church and secular agencies. COMMIT's purpose is to equip persons and groups with skills to change social structures and liberate and empower people. Among the agency's projects have been organizing white suburban churches for awareness and action training on issues of racism, supporting antiwar action and women's issues, conducting continuing education programs for clergy, and supervising seminary students in field work. COMMIT would like to spend less time maintaining established groups and more time on unpopular issues such as peace and black empowerment. COMMIT is an example of an increasing number of specialized agencies offering resources needed by churches; an exponent of the

action-reflection training method; and a case study in the entre-
prenurial style of religious leadership. (For fuller discussion, see
Chapter 3.)

CONGREGATION SOLEL in Highland Park, Illinois, began in
1954 as a study group of twenty to thirty families who had
recently moved from a Reformed temple on Chicago's South
Side. From within the Reform tradition, Congregation Solel has
helped its members own their Jewish identity and heritage,
relating the Torah to the difficult issues of public life. Recogniz-
ing the need for a formal congregation, in 1957 the group called
Rabbi Arnold Wolf. Solel's central goal is to help congregants
search out, relate to, and act upon their Jewishness. "The Solel
Way" is defined as "a search without the promise of an answer."
The search manifests itself in the congregation's serious emphasis on Jewish studies, including classes for all ages in the Torah,
Jewish history and tradition, and Hebrew. There are also
courses on literary analysis of the Old Testament and Yoga.
Contemporary social problems, such as Vietnam and racism are
discussed, and attempts to deal with them have been made. The
search also manifests itself in the group's expression "experiment and risk," which indicates the encouragement of lay responsibility and experimentation, even at the risk of failure. In
order to preserve the integrity of congregational life, the membership is limited to 425 families. The current budget is approximately $250,000.

EARTHLIGHT is in Boston, Massachusetts and was founded
by five persons in February 1971 to make video tape equipment
and skills more widely available and to inform people of the
possibility of Cable Television for public access broadcasting.
The group exists around the purpose of using video tape as a
method for popular education and community organization.
Earthlight is interested in being in touch with groups in the
community who wish to develop alternative life styles, political
and social action, but who do not have the resources themselves
to gain access to mass media such as commercial television and

newspapers. It also intends to be a community of economic and emotional support realizing in its own life the awareness and values it would communicate through video tape. The medium or services that it offers carries the message of its own life style and values. There are currently six members, all white, in the collective which meets once a week to plan and implement video tape projects financed by members' earnings from other jobs. The group goal is "facilitating communication in the community, while supporting, reinforcing and criticizing other ideals and awareness."

EMMAUS HOUSE began in New York City in 1966 when six people decided to form a collective with two goals: exploring new forms in worship and community life, and providing a center for discussion and implementation of alternatives to the present social structure. As an alternative community, Emmaus House has experimented with liturgy and an intentional living community and work collective. As a center of Catholic action and New Left activities, it has a strong commitment to the transformation and humanization of society on an explicitly Christian basis. The community has generated and attempted to live out a radical political critique of American society from this religious base, nurturing a wide variety of ideas and programs on a small budget varying from $12,000 to $29,000 a year. Among Emmaus House activities are: *The Bread is Rising,* an occasional journal; a neighborhood day school; *The People's Yellow Pages,* a telephone directory of legal services; free breakfast and free clothing programs. New values have arisen from the thought and work of Emmaus House, such as a "new asceticism" and service without paternalism to the East Harlem community in which Emmaus House is located. A wide variety of activities aimed at social change has been initiated by former members. The group participates in a larger informal community of support for religious and social dissent, having sponsored projects such as the Harrisburg Defense Committee for the legal defense of the Berrigans and others in 1970, and Vocations for Social Change, an information service on alternative employment opportunities and services. There are currently twelve resident members.

FOR LOVE OF CHILDREN

In 1965 a group of volunteers working at Washington D.C.'s Junior Village developed a concern about Washington's Child Welfare System. They wanted to change the system to remove as few children as possible from their parents, to provide more than mere custodial care for children who required placement in institutions, and to help as many dependent children as possible move into adoptive homes. They wanted to make sure that the Child Welfare System was alert to the needs of every child within it.

FLOC was established and is supported by local churches, the Church of the Savior contributing the most substantial aid. The mission group interviewed for this study came to pattern its inner life after the discipline of the Church of the Savior and in 1969 became a mission group of that Church. After a twelve week orientation course, persons join mission task groups of 5–15 members and with the aid of a staff member enter upon a program of political advocacy in regard to the welfare system, the establishment of foster homes, reading programs for foster children, the development of a learning center for children with special learning problems. The theological assumptions and Christian life style of the Church of the Savior enable the mission group to combine social political advocacy, the meeting of specific human needs, and the building of their own support community.

GLIDE MEMORIAL UNITED METHODIST CHURCH, founded in 1929, is an interracial congregation in downtown San Francisco which is nationally known for the excitement of its worship and for its involvement with and service to oppressed groups in the urban area. The church is one of three interrelated organizations: Glide Foundation, the funding organization which supports the basic costs of the programs; the Glide Urban Center, which operates specialized ministries to "out groups" of society (ethnic and racial groups, the poor, women, homosexuals, and the elderly); and Glide Memorial Church itself. Under the leadership of the black pastor, Cecil Williams, who arrived in 1967, the worship became "a far-out kind of celebration including a rock band, light show, and highly nontraditional liturgy," according to the researcher. Glide Foundation is an example of the creative use of endowment, enabling the church to take risks and move into controversial areas. The church is also a rare example of the successful transition from a white to a predominantly black congregation in which the active involvement and leadership of both groups is sustained. All races, classes, and ages are represented among the members of the church and the thousands more who participate in Glide's activities. The budget is around $60,000. (For fuller discussion, see chapter 3.)

HAVURAT SHALOM, in Somerville, Massachusetts, is a community seminary which offers an alternative to the traditional modes of Jewish study carried out in seminaries, Hebrew colleges, and universities. Founded by Rabbi Arthur Green and twenty students and faculty in the fall of 1968, it emphasizes the religious quest above the dispassionate search for knowledge. There are no fixed lines separating teacher and pupil—all are fellow learners and teachers in community. The community is open to other religious traditions as well, and experiences the full range of worship and prayer of the Jewish tradition. It is described by Rabbi Stephen Learner as combining intensity of feeling and unembarrassed exuberance with study in the modern vein. Havurat or fellowships of scholars evidently have existed since Talmudic times, and the community also owes part of its inspiration to conversations between Rabbi Green and Father Daniel Berrigan. There are currently twenty members in the community, who pay $350 a year for maintenance of the house.

The major goal of JEWISH PARENTS INSTITUTE in Detroit, Michigan is to create a positive Jewish identity by making its members aware of their tie to Jewish tradition, history, ethics, and culture. Founded in 1947, the distinctive feature of its program is the emphasis on secularism as a viable alternative for Jews. The Institute founded and operates a private school for Jewish children, who begin their study of Judaism with Bible stories, study Maimonides and Halevy by the time they are eleven, and conclude with the study of secular Judaism before they graduate from the school at thirteen. Parents help develop the curriculum and set educational standards in an open learning atmosphere. They also hold social activities, including dance, theatre, and singing, and celebrate some Jewish holidays. Jewish Parents Institute intends to provide an alternative to the three traditional Jewish groups, stressing a supportive community, a positive Jewish identity, and guidelines for social action. Over 200 families belong to the Institute, contributing an annual budget of $35,000.

JOINT HEALTH VENTURE, in Hollywood, California, began in 1969 in a living room conversation among fifteen men and women who were committed to finding a way to take positive action about the health crisis in their community. Sparked by such leaders as John Wagner, Jr., of the National Council of Churches, and Dr. Herbert Dougherty, a sociologist active in community affairs, the group has grown to over 100 volunteer members of all races who covenant together to improve the quality of health care, beginning in their own community of Hollywood. The program is organized around five themes. The first is advocacy of equal opportunities for growth for all hospital workers, regardless of sex, color, educational background, or professional status. The second is consciousness raising in the Hollywood community about health needs and resources, often by educational programs in local churches. The third is to provide direct health care services through churches in communisties where such services are not otherwise available. The fourth is advocacy of system-wide health care planning that takes into account the needs and resources of all sections of the community. The fifth aim is reflection on and evaluation of Joint Health Venture itself, including theological reflection and articulation of the group's assumptions and program.

KING'S TEMPLE is an independent Pentecostal church in Seattle, Washington, founded in 1963 by the Rev. Charlotte Baker. It is an example of the revivalist churches that emphasize a church order founded entirely on prophecy. The worship is enthusiastic and orderly, with choir, orchestra, praying in tongues, and frequent use of traditional biblical language. The doctrines of Providence and the Call are central to the life of the 350-member church. The will of God, known through prophecy, orders both congregational and individual life. Members report deliverance from difficult personal problems, and are certain of God's call for their lives. A vision of the Glory of the Lord filling the earth inspires home and foreign mission activities initiated and supported by the congregation. The church looks forward to spending more of its income on mission than on church maintenance. The 350 members are mostly middle-class, which illustrates the growth of the Pentecostal movement among groups traditionally served by mainline Protestant churches. (For fuller description see Chapter 1.)

KOINONIA MISSIONARY BAPTIST CHURCH, Gary, Indiana, is a black, independent Baptist church affiliated with the National Progressive Baptist Convention. The Rev. Thomas L. Brown has organized the church around the idea of *koinonia* expressed both in its own fellowship and in community service. The church has grown rapidly since its founding in 1971 to its present 400 members. After acquiring the necessary equipment, meeting space, and staff, it moved on to a variety of community action programs, including placing 146 students in colleges (and assisting them financially when necessary), and establishing the first Opportunities Industrialization Center in Gary. The current budget is around $50,000. Church programs, such as a family revival series, an ecumenical workshop, and workshops with visiting preachers and theologians, are well attended. Most people join Koinonia because they want to work for the community. The emphasis on *koinonia* as the integrating theological principle allows this congregation to combine a Baptist interpretation of the faith with effective social action in the community. Koinonia demonstrates the power of the Church in the black community and the authority of the black ministry.

LIGHTHOUSE RANCH is a fast growing young Jesus commune in Lolita, California, founded in 1970. It teaches the total identification of life and thought with Christ as Lord. Many of the 130 members, who range in age mainly from the mid-teens to the late twenties, come to the ranch with problems related to life direction, family, or drugs. Participation in the structured round of prayers, singing, witnessing together, common meals, shared work, and church services, and the training and preaching of the leader, the Rev. James Durkin, make sense to these young people. For them, Lighthouse Ranch fulfills their needs for identity, direction, and stable structures for their lives. The structure has plenty of room for fun, for loving, and for joyful relationships. The Lighthouse lifestyle is intentionally modest, and various projects (clean-up crews, a crafts shop, publication of shopping news, and selling baked goods) help bring in necessary funds. The group believes that the solution of social problems is to be found in God's Kingdom, in which Christians can participate now. There is little tolerance for "dead" churches, but the Lighthouse sends out missionaries to secular communes and has begun a storefront mission in town. Members believe that "in everything, God gives the plans and shows the group how to carry them out. The believers' duties are not to make long-term plans, but to deny oneself and to live the Word in fellowship with God and each other twenty-four hours a day." (For fuller discussion, see chapter 6.)

LINCOLN SQUARE SYNAGOGUE, in New York City, founded in 1964, is a powerful example in our study of a group centered around a charismatic leader. Rabbi Steven Riskin combines an extraordinary ability to elicit admiration and devotion from his 350-family members with unusual skill and charisma in teaching the Orthodox Jewish tradition. "The rabbi is something that God has given to us," say members. The new synagogue, built at a cost of over a million dollars in 1971, is constructed in the round, seating 500 people in an intimate setting which reflects the rabbi's vision of a close and caring community. "Care," "love," and "concern" are the important words in the common life of the synagogue. The enthusiastic singing is led by the clapping (and even jumping) rabbi. Feeling that Jewish survival depends on a return to orthodoxy, retaining the full content of the Law, but adapting it to modern forms, Rabbi Riskin expounds the Jewish tradition as religious experience. The tradition is taught in heavily attended adult education courses, nursery and primary religious schools, and a Hebrew high school. Participating in their orthodox tradition, members can feel part of a people whose history spans thousands of years. (For fuller discussion, see chapter 4.)

NEW COMMUNITY PROJECTS, INC., the most recent project of Interseminarian, in Boston, aims to deal directly with the increasingly serious interest in alternative forms of intimate community and extended family. The first Interseminarian project, begun by Harvard Divinity School student Peter Calloway in 1967, was Project Place, which provided counseling and temporary lodging for troubled young people. The founders, themselves alienated from contemporary social structures, were able to help teenagers suffering from that same alienation. New Community Projects has evolved out of Interseminarian staff members' experience with community life into a counseling and consulting service for communes. Interseminarian is a remarkably successful attempt to build a complex social service organization around countercultural values and aims, while "making it" in the straight world. The group shares all responsibilities; the paid staff (at times numbering as many as fifty) live on $5,000 a year each; and an impressive array of professionals and nonprofessionals volunteers to help in different projects. As a result, Interseminarian can deliver $750,000 worth of services for one-third the cost. The community's personal and professional life is joined—many live in communes, and all enjoy monthly weekends at a New Hampshire farm. (For fuller discussion, see chapter 6.)

THE NOW CHURCH, in San Jose, California, began in 1969 through the efforts of the Rev. Peter Koopman, a Presbyterian minister who was called by his denomination to organize a new church in the area. However, the fifteen to twenty original members and the current forty active members characterize themselves as "church drop-outs," and the house church they evolved is not a Presbyterian church. It is an informal, intimate community that stresses the participation and leadership of all its members, and considers its part-time minister to be more of a facilitator and resource person than a pastor to whom the community looks for its dominant leadership. The church has specialized in experimenting in worship, and the "open, informal, two-hour happening" on Sunday morning "always includes frank discussion of controversial events, emphasis on sensitivity and awareness, and continual opportunities for individual participation." It struggles with the typical problems of house churches—a minimal budget ($4,000), and the need to institutionalize for continuity and stability without sacrificing spontaneity and intimacy. But it meets the needs of the minority of persons (in this case, middle-class and mostly, but not exclusively, white) who want a church community, but not the life of the typical Protestant congregation.

ONAGER FAMILY in Boston, Massachusetts consists of six adults and three children ranging in ages from an infant baby girl to 30 years of age. Onager Family intends to be a commune living out of a shared life pattern that provides support for each other as human beings and demonstrates alternative living styles in this culture. The reduced consumption of material goods, recycling and conservation are important goals and focuses of group activities. In addition, members of the group work in a number of alternative education projects. The group emphasizes common meetings with discussions about issues in group life and projects. There is interest in egalitarian and flexible sex roles, open education, shared parenting, and increased freedom of activity for children as well as ecology and non–capitalistic economic system. The religious content of the group is only implicit. Institutionalized religion as such is of little interest to group members.

OPEN END, in San Rafael, California, is a nonresidential community that seeks to offer "alternative" and deeper levels of community to middle-class suburbanites. Founded in 1969 by an Episcopal priest and his wife, the Rev. Frank and Barbara Potter, Open End aims to help its members arrive at greater self-awareness and sensitivity to others, and to meet their need for an intimate community. The insights and methods of the human potential and sensitivity training movements are used to address traditionally religious issues of community, self-identity, vocation, and the shaping of values. While the issues are religious, the group searches for new language and new methods with which to address them. The community provides a wide variety of programs, from hiking to encounter groups; issues a monthly newsletter; and offers consultant services for groups interested in forming new communities. Monthly dues paid by the 280 members provide a budget of $20–25,000 to support the program and the minimal paid leadership, whose primary responsibilities are generating new program ideas and encouraging and training members to lead the workshops, laboratory experiences, and recreational activities that appeal to them. Trustees elected by the members have final responsibility for all policy designs. Open End offers a new way of updating the traditional role of the local congregation as a center for community social life. (For fuller discussion, see chapter 3.)

PRINCE OF PEACE AMERICAN LUTHERAN CHURCH is a suburban congregation in Burnsville, Minnesota which has grown rapidly from 200 members at its founding in 1963 to 1800 current members by responding to the needs for social relationships, communal support, and community building that still exist in fast growing suburbia. Its current budget is around $100,000. Having outgrown its original sanctuary, the congregation decided to locate the church at the crossroads of two major highways, as part of a complex including a hospital, nursing home, residential building for senior citizens, health care center, geriatrics and youth services center, and low and moderate income housing. The church hopes in this way to provide extensive ministries in partnership with the community facilities. The values and beliefs of the members are orthodox and theologically grounded. One member summed up the church's goals as "to be a part of God's will, to care for His people, to respond to His grace, to find and help others find Peace, Joy, and Justice."

PROJECT CHALLENGE, in Avalon, California, was founded in 1962 by a group of eight ministers and laymen to bring college-age young people to Christ through the evangelical Christian churches in southern California. A board of twelve directors and a full-time executive director sponsor a one-week camp in the fall, a weekend Winter Convocation, a newspaper, and a number of mission work camps in Mexico, and on Indian reservations and orphanages in this country. The program reaches around 400 college-age and older adults each year. A coffee house and a drug counseling program are also related to the organization. The budget of around $25,000 is raised from local churches and by individual contributors who pledge $100 each and attend an annual dinner in support of the program. Project Challenge is an example of lay supported and initiated evangelical efforts to reach unchurched young adults with a conservative Christian message. The program is traditional in content and format, although it intends to identify with young adult language, values, and lifestyle. The particular emphasis is a challenge to a "Christian Career," which does not necessarily mean the ordained ministry, but a life of Christian service.

RANCHO COLORADO is a planned-unit development in the process of construction in a suburban area east of Oakland, California. The community began in discussions among several members of a United Church of Christ house church in Concord, California. After camping retreats together in 1970, six of the families began discussing with the pastor the possibility of creating together a new kind of community. As the discussions continued, they conceived of the idea of buying property together and building houses for each family unit as well as a community building for the total group use. The group formed a partnership for the purpose of securing $150,000 to buy the property and to negotiate with local planning commissions for approval to build. Initial local community resistance to their novel idea seems to be dissipating. The basic purpose of the group is to build a community, meaning both a setting for families to enrich each other by mutual caring as well as the actual physical construction.

Two groups in New York City who are members of the INTERNATIONAL NEW THOUGHT ALLIANCE were studied jointly. The groups are THE RELIGIOUS SCIENCE MINISTRY of Dr. Raymond Charles Barker, and THE UNITY CHURCH in Manhattan. Both trace their lineage to Phineas Parkhurst Quimby, who began using mesmerism in Boston in the 1840s and 1850s. By 1860 he had decided that the use of Mesmer's technique was not necessary and began teaching the spiritual nature of the universe and of man. Mr. Quimby healed Mary Baker Eddy, who in turn began the Christian Science Church. One of Mrs. Eddy's early colleagues was Emma Curtis Hopkins, founder of the Christian Science Seminary in Chicago. Mr. and Mrs. Charles Fillmore, the founders of Unity Church, graduated from that seminary. Religious Science, the particular tradition Dr. Barker represents, began later, in 1918.

New Thought teachings are known and practiced by millions of Americans—who may or may not be formal members of other church bodies—through such publications as the *Daily Word* and through the work of the various branches of New Thought. New Thought teaches the application of spiritual principles to everyday reality and problems through meditation or scientific prayer. People are encouraged to believe that God will reward them according to their ability to believe in the spiritual nature of reality. "God is Mind" is the fundamental tenet; God is all-presence, all-power, and all-substance. One who understands and believes this with singlemindedness should be able to demonstrate the power of God in all of life, from one's financial situation to one's physical health. However, the discipline of realizing the essential nature of life and God may take years to accomplish. Dr. Barker's radio ministry reaches several thousands each week. The Unity congregation totals 700 members. Both groups are middle-class, and predominantly, though not exclusively, white.

The Roman Catholic ST. FRANCIS DE SALES CATHEDRAL is located in the heart of Oakland, California, with parish boundaries which reach from the ghetto to the upper-class residential area above Oakland. When St. Francis de Sales was designated the cathedral of the new diocese, a new pastor was appointed in 1968 who decided to share policy making administration of the $40,000 budget and parish responsibilities with the two associate pastors and the four nuns who taught in the parish school. This team decided on Sunday worship services and the school as the highest priorities. One associate pastor has developed a contemporary service called "Creative Celebration," in which the choir, an instrumental ensemble, and the congregation provide music in every idiom from Bach to rock. The verbal, musical, and visual elements of the service are planned to reinforce central themes, such as "humor," "play," and "faces in the revolution." Multi-racial, standing-room-only crowds of over 1,000 mean that parishioners have to arrive at the cathedral before 10 A.M. in order to get seats at the 10:30 Mass. St. Francis de Sales brings sophisticated contemporary resources to the service of traditional ministries, primarily clergy-led. It is an example of a successful urban, Catholic parish in the vitality of its liturgy, the compassion and effectiveness of its social services, and the creative teaching in its parochial school. (For fuller description, see chapter 3.)

ST. FRANCIS PRESBYTERIAN CHURCH, a 150-member liberal Protestant congregation in Fort Worth, Texas, was founded in 1965 by people who wanted "something different than the prestigious new church in suburbia." Much of the congregation's effort since that time has been spent in identifying what that "something different" might be. Placing high value on its role as pathfinder and innovator, St. Francis Church has struggled with its identity and purpose, and has assimilated many of the insights of the church renewal literature in its life. The congregation is primarily, but not exclusively, white and operates a budget of $30,000 a year. It has placed heavy emphasis on human relations training, using members' skills to help it develop into an open community in which participants can express their opinions freely, manage conflict, and handle decision-making problems. One difficult decision was to postpone building plans in favor of remaining a house church. St. Francis's high member discipline has also been expressed in community social action projects, in which members engage both as individuals and as congregational groups. (For fuller description see chapter 1.)

ST. JOHN'S ABBEY, in Collegeville, Minnesota, is the largest Benedictine abbey in the world, with 320 members, 170 of whom live at the abbey. The rest serve in parishes, chaplaincies, and other apostolates around the world. The abbey was founded in 1856 with five members for the purpose of caring for the spiritual needs of German-speaking Catholics. The program has grown as steadily as the membership, and now includes missions around the world, the development of St. John's University (within which the abbey is located), the Institute for Ecumenical and Cultural Research, a radio station, and other mission enterprises. The abbey is perhaps best known for its work on liturgical reform and renewal. Monks of the abbey did much of the writing of the liturgical reforms adopted by the Second Vatican Council. The purpose of St. John's Abbey is "to be a permanent yet flexible Christian community of prayer and service within which the individual members will be assisted in finding God in the service He renders through the community to the church and to society in accord with the spirit of the Rule of St. Benedict." Each Benedictine abbey is substantially independent, and the monks are proud of their independence, their history, tradition, and identity. The community's budget is integrated into the university's, and is supported largely by the income of monks serving in parishes and teaching positions. Monks who are professors at the university, for example, return 80 percent of their salary to the abbey.

ST. JUSTIN'S CONVENT, in New Haven, Connecticut, was founded in 1972 by six sisters of Notre Dame as a residential community to facilitate their summer study at nearby state

college campuses. The group formed both for the practical reason of providing a living arrangement for summer study and for
the underlying goal of deepening the awareness of community.
Such informal and temporary communities of monks and especially nuns are not uncommon. They represent an increasing
freedom to experiment with intimate community, testing the
flexibility and freedom of the monastic tradition to meet the
needs for closeness and support that are so urgent and widespread in our fragmented culture. Liturgies and celebrations
held in the apartment provide the high points of group life.

SH'MA, a biweekly journal of opinion and dialectic relating
Jewish values and tradition to social concerns, was founded by
Eugene Borowitz in 1970. As subscriptions and contributions
came pouring in, the journal became established in the Jewish
community. Sh'ma is an example of a community without organization. Borowitz, its founder, editor, and guiding force, is a
volunteer, as are contributing editors from the Jewish intellectual community. Sixty-five hundred subscribers constitute the
larger community related to Sh'ma. Borowitz attempts to provide an open forum for hammering out issues from many different points of view and addressing the loneliness of the thoughtful Jew who may be alienated from participation in his local
synagogue. Representing diverse viewpoints, the eight-page
journal provides an opportunity for sharp but appropriate Jewish dialectic. Sharing the wide interest in communications
among religious groups, Borowitz has demonstrated that the
publication of a journal can also be a method for building community. (For fuller description, see chapter 3.)

SPIRIT OF '76 in Boston, Massachusetts began in early 1971.
Four persons were connected with Old West Church, two of
them being ministerial students. Four others worked at the
Shrine Burn Center in Boston. There are currently six men, five
women, and one child in the group. The age range is 21–35
years. The group purchased a house in October of 1971 to
implement their initial goal of becoming an alternate extended

family. In the group interview the group expressed the goal of learning to live together and learning to be comfortable with each other. Spirit of 76 focuses its group activities around weekly meetings and common meals. Some persons have wanted the community to become involved in political action in the larger community but this has not materialized. The group is an example of the hunger for intimate relationships and the conscious desire to build a living arrangement which facilitates the values of the extended family but in a modern urban setting. They wish to demonstrate an alternative to the nuclear family. Values and goals beyond that are not spelled out. In many ways, to paraphrase McLuhan, "the community itself is the message."

THE STUDY AND DISCUSSION GROUP, in Springfield, Massachusetts, was organized by thirty-six lay Roman Catholics in 1968 to realize a more intimate community of faith than they believed was possible in the traditional parish structure. The group was able to secure the presence of a liturgical leader, but the bishop refused its request for the assignment of a priest. One of the members was then ordained in a Byzantine rite. In 1969, the group developed a formal proposal to be recognized as a nonterritorial parish. The goals of the proposal included genuine personal involvement in an intimate community of faith, a closer relationship with a priest, adapting the liturgy to make it more meaningful, and social action in the community. The ecclesiastical authorities turned down the proposal and suggested the group disband and the members return to their original parishes, which they refused to do. The group contained eighteen members at the time of the interview, all white, middleclass, of a variety of ethnic origins, as was the original group. The Study and Discussion Group is an example of what seems to be a surprisingly widespread phenomenon of lay initiated informal groups emerging from or coexisting uneasily on the periphery of synagogues and Protestant and Catholic churches. They have in common a desire for more intimacy of community, vitality of worship and commonality of purpose and action than they can realize in the regular parish or congregational structure. Their fate depends to a fair extent on the behavior of clerical authorities toward them. Sometimes they are able to call their own professional leadership and grow into a new congregation, as happened with Congregation Solel. Sometimes they continue on the margins of an established congregation, furnishing an uncomfortable but challenging force for renewal. And at other times they find it difficult to survive in the face of active clerical disapproval, as seems to have happened here.

TAIL OF THE TIGER is a meditative community in Barnet, Vermont, dedicated to understanding and following the teachings of Tibetan Buddhism. The community was begun in 1970 under the leadership of Chogyam Trungpa Rimpoche, formerly abbot of a group of Tibetan monasteries, who emphasizes relating the teachings of Tibetan Buddhism to specific circumstances of American life. Tail of the Tiger has grown steadily, and now includes twenty-four permanent members and a number of visitors, of whom a large majority are Jewish, and some black. The annual expenses of the community are around $20,000. In addition to the thrice daily meditations, the community's primary focus, there are a craft center and an occasional journal. In its organization the group combines an easy corporate democracy with the direct personal authority of the guru, when he is present. Group goals center around practical matters, such as work assignments. Each individual has his or her own spiritual journey, with no goal save the path itself. Members are together not because of warm feelings for each other, but because of their mutual interest in Tibetan Buddhism. Outsiders are neither excluded nor welcomed. As one member said, "Nothing is to be taken seriously, save the teachings and death." (For fuller discussion, see chapter 4.)

TEEN CHALLENGE, of Cucamonga, California, is an evangelical Christian facility for the treatment of drug abuse. Inspired by the experiences reported in *The Cross and the Switchblade*, it began in 1965 to develop supportive therapy in a semirestricted environment based on the principles of total abstinence and "distinctly Christian psychological premises." To be admitted, addicts must have "an honest desire for a changed lifestyle, a drug abuse or addiction problem so acute that functioning in open society is unrealistic, and approval by an ex-addict screening committee." Those admitted spend the first three months in the more restricted Cucamonga setting, and the next three months and whatever additional time is needed for resocialization in the *Riverside House*. Each setting houses around sixteen people, of a variety of racial and economic backgrounds. The rehabilitation is supported by individual contributions and local governments, which pay for the treatment of juveniles. Teen Challenge is strongly evangelical and Pentecostal in its approach, offering a total lifestyle and supportive community and relationship with local churches to replace the environments and behavior patterns of drug use.

VANGUARD MAGAZINE, Toronto, Canada, is the communication arm of a group of Neo-Calvinists, who are committed to a renaissance of Calvinist thought in public life, including politics, art, and the university. This "radical Christian movement" was inspired by a turn of the century Dutch reformer who stressed the idea that "life is religion" and that the Christian way of life integrates all human activities. Netherlanders immigrating to North America after World War II started a number of communal expressions of this reformational movement. Largely ignored by liberal groups and an object of controversy in evangelical circles, the movement is a combination of biblical solidarity mixed with sometimes "radical" strategies for witnessing. Wholehearted embracing of cultural life, a strong emphasis on *task* and on a convenantal, responsive understanding of religion, have led the group to a struggle to restructure the whole of society. Ways of working on this aim include such organizations as the 4000-member Christian Labour Association of Canada, direct action programs, and the multi-discipline analysis and research efforts undertaken at the Institute for Christian Studies. Vanguard Magazine itself was founded in 1968. Its current subscription list is 2,000. The six person editorial staff operates on a budget of around $20,000.

Appendix B

THE INSEARCH CONFERENCE

The Insearch Project findings were submitted to a group of eighty-two consultants who attended a four-day conference in Chicago in January, 1973. The participants were, as intended, a diverse group. We wanted to create dialogue across the spectrum of religious life in America. So, group members came from every faith within the Judaeo-Christian tradition (with a few outside that tradition) and represented a wide range of occupations, but most prominantly, executives of national church and synagogue organizations. Serious and partially successful attempts were made to balance the dominance of white middle-aged men with non-whites, women, and young people.

The problems facing organized religion were described in the following statement which was displayed in the small group meeting rooms during the conference:

Churches and synagogues appear to be suffering a certain failure of nerve, while at the same time the longing for God and experimentation with religious forms are increasing. If this is so, the urgent need is not only for careful organizational planning, but for a vision, a creative image, within which planning makes sense.

163

The conference was designed so that the participants could encounter one another and the research documentation in order to generate visions of the future of religion which were:

1. True to the best we know of God's love and will;
2. Feasible in terms of our best insights about the nature of contemporary society;
3. Compelling enough to make us work for their realization.

The central task of the conference was to relate information to policy choice. Policy formation requires the making of complex decisions on the basis of incomplete information. It is difficult to bring research to bear on policy decisions. Often the questions a policymaker needs to ask are not the questions the researcher has been able to ask, or else the data are not in a form that can be readily used by the policymaker.

To meet this problem, the conference employed two concepts: pattern recognition and feedback loops. Pattern recognition occurs when a person puts together a number of discrete perceptions into an overall form that makes sense of the separate bits of information. Most of us, most of the time, impose habitual patterns even on unfamiliar data. In order to think seriously about the future of religion, it is necessary to break out of these habitual patterns. Immersion in the unfamiliar allows one to build fresh patterns of seeing. Films, documentaries, case studies, videotapes, and graphics were used to encourage participants to see things in new ways.

The conference also used feedback loops. Conferees were able to ask questions, receive data, reformulate questions, and receive data again. This cycling of information request and responses was built into the conference by means of small group discussions, a videotape feedback process, and even an improvisational theatre group.

The data from our study were introduced to the conference in two ways. First, we let the religious groups studied tell us their own story. The videotaped group interviews provided a means for conferees to participate intimately in the raw and unrehearsed life of the groups. Brief case descriptions and longer case studies like those included in this book helped to put the raw data in historical perspective.

Secondly, we presented quantitative analysis of the data. We used statistical analysis in the light of social science theory to examine the values of the group members, patterns of group beliefs, characteristics of group life, and group strategies for member and world change.

As part of a demanding conference schedule, participants were asked to learn about the future by helping to create it. We attempted to create a conference environment which was as overstimulating, varied, and confusing as we believe the emerging future of our culture will be. We hoped such an environment would encourage the initiative, commitment, and involvement that are required in planning for the future amidst social and cultural change. Thus, the participants themselves added depth and scope to the interpretation of the study findings.

Appendix C

The participants at the Insearch Conference focused much of their energy on how to develop a balanced mission for congregations. Several of the informal discussion groups' reports suggested an increasing pluralism in the church, in which task forces and experiential groups would be related in mission. One group reported as follows:

Faced with a society which is becoming more and more pluralistic and one in which lifestyles are diverging rather than converging, the general opinion of the group is that the church of the future is going to be more and more diverse. Organizationally we can expect more and more churches and groupings of churches, and these will vary in size, in cultural groupings, and in task orientation. At the same time we foresee an increasing number of "para-church" groups which will act as service agencies for the local body.

Additionally, we anticipate that groups will be task- or goal-oriented, and that each group might have a set of well-defined and highly communicable goals. In order to continue to operate as part of a larger body, the group will need adequate and appropriate information about the world in which it is trying to support its membership and toward which it is trying to minister. Whether it will be possible for the group to obtain this information with its own resources, or whether it will look to other special agencies to provide the information remains to be seen. In a society in which means of communication are growing very rapidly, the possibility of the "self-organizing" group is greater than ever.

We already have many instances in our society of special purpose groups, some of them within ecclesiastical structure and some without. In order to be defined as "religious" groups, these special purpose groups must possess certain basic characteristics. They should be biblically rooted and spiritually vital. In other words, they should be carriers of a religious tradition and this religious tradition should be at the core of their being. In time they should see themselves as part of a larger body, looking forward to an international church which is not necessarily related organizationally, but is related through the common tradition.

In order to maintain their vitality, these special purpose religious groups should have a built-in system of self-renewal for each of the local groups. One way of maintaining such self-renewal is to regularly reexamine the goal commitment and task for which the group was originally formed, and to request that each individual recommit himself to the task of the group or help to redefine the task if that is necessary. In many cases it will be appropriate for the group to disband.

In predicting the increasing diversity of groups, we see less need for large hierarchical structures such as are present in some of our denominations. Many of these hierarchical structures have developed as modes of communication rather than modes of authority. In the society toward which we are moving, however, as the sophistication of communication improves, the necessity for communication-oriented hierarchical structures will diminish. This does *not* mean, however, that what are presently small movements (special purpose religious groups) will not develop their own hierarchical structures as they begin to grow. It means only that the *necessity* for doing so will decline.

One group which included some experienced consultants to religious organizations developed specific suggestions for congregational clusters, using the consultants' own past experience in working with such groups.

The central theme that should be incorporated in our proposed religious community is "struggle and celebration." Our ideal vision is a cluster of local congregations working together for specific objectives in an inner city.
The objectives are:
—To create a community in which the needs of each congregation would be served, and to - which each could contribute significantly from its strength;

—To keep openness of organization;

—To collaborate on tasks that would be supportive and aid growth;

—To maintain the independence of each congregation— there would be no intention to merge;

—To live in full acceptance of diverse pluralistic styles;

—To draw strength from diversity, accepting the struggle inherent in the differences;

—To create the sense of a larger family;

—To engage in mission together in order to do more than groups could do separately.
We believe that this cluster of congregations can be effective only if there has been a deep resolve to establish a conventional relationship between strong, viable local churches that represent markedly different styles, constituencies, and liturgical and ecclesiastical traditions. We recommend that it consist of four churches: Roman Catholic, black Protestant, Pentecostal, mainline Protestant. The covenant should include these elements:
—Decision to proceed in any action only after comprehensive opportunities for understanding and input in each church;

—Agreement to proceed in the name of the cluster only if all churches agree to do so;

—Candid presentation of all issues so they may be debated and resolved without risking the sense of "diverse unity" of the cluster.

A third group summed up in a more formal statement their faith in the possibility of relating religious tradition, mission, and personal experience:

Today many congregations, groups, and movements are emerging outside and inside the mainline churches—groups with particular religious experiences and commitments: Pentecostal fellowships, communes, personal growth groups, spiritual quest communities, ethnic groups, communities concentrating on particular tasks of social care and social change. We have been introduced to a sample of such groups through the research for this conference, and we sense the presence of God's Spirit in them.

We believe that a congregation of God's people should reach out to include such diversity within a large unity where there can be mutual enrichment and correction—often, no doubt, through tension and conflict.

The congregation meets in open inclusive gathering to hear the story and to celebrate it. [It] seeks to dedicate itself to mission in the world in "task forces" committed to social justice and the struggles for racial equality, liberation of oppressed peoples, peace, and institutional change in persons. [It] seeks deeper levels of personal commitment and mutual growth in small groups—"experiential and experimental groups."

We are affirming the need for congregations inclusive enough to be open to people at many different stages of growth and commitment—yet committed to providing living illustrations of the promises of God. These congregations will serve a dual function: to internalize the faith through the richness of God's grace, and to provide the strength to relate discipleship to the profound needs of God's world.

Notes

CHAPTER 1

1. George Gallup, Jr. and John O. Davies, III, *Religion in America, 1971* (Princeton, New Jersey: Gallup International, Inc., 1971).
2. *Giving USA: A Complication of Facts & Trends on American Philanthropy for the Year 1971,* 1972 edition. (New York: American Association of Fund-Raising Counsel, 1972), p. 6.
3. Douglas W. Johnson and George W. Cornell, *Punctured Preconceptions, What North Americans Think About the Church* (New York: Friendship Press, 1972), p. 119.

CHAPTER 2

1. Alfred Schutz, *The Phenomenology of the Social World* (Evanston, Illinois: Northwestern University Press, 1967).
2. Michael Polanyi, *Personal Knowledge: Toward a Post Critical Philosophy* (New York: Harper Torch Books, 1964), p. 90.
3. Emile Durkheim, *The Elementary Forms of Religious Life* (London: Collier-Macmillan Publishers, 1961).
4. Thomas Luckmann, *Invisible Religion* (New York: Macmillan Publishing Co., 1967), p. 3.
5. *Ibid.,* p. 66.
6. *Ibid.,* p. 81.
7. Winthrop Hudson, *Religion in America* (New York: Charles Scribner's Sons, 1965), p. 13.
8. *Ibid.,* p. 18.
9. Thomas F. O'Dea, *The Sociology of Religion* (Englewood Cliffs, New Jersey: Prentice Hall, 1966), pp. 36–55.

10. Alvin Toffler, *Future Shock* (New York: Random House, 1970), p. 290.
11. *Ibid.,* p. 37.
12. Thomas Luckmann, *Invisible Religion* (New York: Macmillan Publishing Company, 1967), pp. 97–99.
13. Saul Bellow, *Mr. Sammler's Planet* (Greenwich, Connecticut: Fawcett Publications, Inc., 1970), p. 212.
14. Erik H. Erikson, *Young Man Luther* (New York: W.W. Norton & Co., 1962), p. 19.
15. Alvin Toffler, *op. cit.,* pp. 196, 278.
16. Thomas Luckmann, *op. cit.,* pp. 91, 97.
17. Alvin Gouldner, *The Coming Crisis in Western Sociology* (New York: Basic Books, 1970), p. 24.
18. *Ibid.,* pp. 85–86.
19. Gerry and Elizabeth Jud, *Training in the Art of Love* (Philadelphia: United Church Press, 1973).
20. Milton Rokeach, *The Nature of Human Values* (New York: The Free Press, 1973), p. 18.
21. *Ibid.,* p. 18.
22. *Ibid.,* pp. 12–13.
23. Louis E. Raths, Merrill Harmin, Sidney B. Simon, *Values and Teaching* (Columbus, Ohio: Charles E. Merrill Publishing Co., 1966), p. 27.
24. *Ibid.,* p. 30.
25. Harold Garfinkel, *Studies in Ethnomethodology* (Englewood Cliffs, New Jersey: Prentice Hall, 1967), p. 96.
26. *Ibid.,* p. 55.
27. Merton Strommen, Milo L. Brekke, Ralph C. Underwager, Arthur L. Johnson, *A Study of Generations* (Minneapolis, Minnesota: Augsburg Publishing House, 1972).
28. Abraham Maslow, *The Further Reaches of Human Nature* (New York: Viking Press, 1971), pp. 72, 79.
29. *Ibid.,* p. 6.
30. *Ibid.,* p. 10.

CHAPTER 3

1. Martin Marty, "The Insearch Groups: Historical Analysis," available at The Institute for Advanced Pastoral Studies, 380 Lone Pine Road, Bloomfield Hills, Michigan 48013.

CHAPTER 4

1. Alfred North Whitehead, *Science and the Modern World* (London: Mentor Books, 1925).
2. Emile Durkheim, *The Elementary Forms of Religious Life* (New York: Collier Books, 1961).
3. Warren G. Bennis, *Changing Organizations* (New York: McGraw-Hill, 1966), p. 12.
4. William Schutz, *The Interpersonal Underworld* (Cupertino, Ca.: Science & Behavior Books, Inc., 1967).
5. Jacob Needleman, *The New Religion* (New York: Harper and Row, 1971).
6. Urban T. Holmes, *The Future Shape of Ministry* (New York: Seabury Press, 1971), pp. 92–3.

CHAPTER 5

1. Charles Glock and Rodney Stark, *Christian Beliefs and Anti-Semitism* (New York: Harper and Row, 1965).
2. Jeffrey Hadden, *The Gathering Storm in the Churches* (New York: Doubleday and Company, 1970), p. 111.
3. Martin Marty, "The Insearch Groups: Historical Analysis," available from the Institute for Advanced Pastoral Studies, 380 Lone Pine Road, Bloomfield Hills, Michigan 48013.
4. Carl Jung, *Man and His Symbols* (London: Aldus Books, Ltd., 1964), p. 161ff.
5. Milton Rokeach, *Value Survey, 1967,* distributed by Halgren Test, 873 Persimmon Avenue, Sunnyvale, California 94087.
6. Hadley Cantril, *The Pattern of Human Concerns* (New Brunswick, New Jersey: Rutgers University Press, 1966), p. 23.
7. Abraham Maslow, *Toward a Psychology of Being* (Princeton, New Jersey: D. Van Nostrand Company, Inc., 1968).
8. Donald E. Spiegel, "Spiegel Personality Inventory," Veterans Administration Center, Los Angeles, California, 1972.
9. George Gallup, Jr. and John O. Davies, III, *Religion in America, 1971* (Princeton, New Jersey: The Gallup Opinion Index Report, 70, 1971).

CHAPTER 6

1. Dean Kelley, *Why Conservative Churches Are Growing* (New York: Harper and Row, 1972).
2. *Ibid.*, p. 79.
3. Kristen Wenzl, "The Religious Belief Systems: A Further Refinement on the Defined Relationship Between Religion and Society" in *Sociological Analysis* 32, n.1 (1971), pp. 45–61.
4. Carl Rogers, *On Becoming a Person* (Boston: Houghton Mifflin Company, 1961), p. 115ff.
5. Dr. O.J. Harvey, Department of Psychology, University of Colorado at Boulder, and Dr. David Hunt, Ontario Institute for Studies in Education, Toronto.

CHAPTER 7

1. Gibson Winter, *The Suburban Captivity of the Churches* (Garden City, N.Y.: Doubleday & Co., Inc., 1961), pp. 20–21.
2. Colin Williams, *The Missionary Structure of the Congregation* (New York: Friendship Press, 1970).
3. Gibson Winter, *The Suburban Captivity of the Churches* (New York: Doubleday and Company, 1961).
4. Pierre Berton, *The Comfortable Pew* (New York: J.B. Lippincott, Co., 1965).
5. Jeffrey K. Hadden, *The Gathering Storm in the Churches* (New York: Doubleday and Company, 1970), p. 111.
6. *Ibid.*, p. 251.
7. *Ibid.*, p. 74.
8. *Ibid.*, p. 74.
9. Williams Watts and Lloyd A. Free, *State of the Nation* (New York: Universe Books, 1973).
10. *Ibid.*, p. 20ff.
11. *Ibid.*, p. 28.
12. *Ibid.*, p. 247.
13. *Ibid.*, p. 257.
14. James H. Leuba, *The Psychological Study of Religion; Its Origin, Its Function, Its Future* (New York: Macmillan, 1912).
15. Orlo Strunk, *Readings in the Psychology of Religion* (Nashville, Tn.: Abingdon Press, 1959).

16. Wayne E. Oates, *The Psychology of Religion* (Waco, Texas: Word, Inc., 1973), pp. 58–59.
17. R.D. Laing, *The Politics of Experience* (New York: Ballantine Books, 1967).
18. Abraham Maslow, *Toward a Psychology of Being,* 2nd ed. (New York: Van Nostrand and Reinhold, 1968); and *Farther Reaches of Human Nature* (New York: Viking Press, 1971).
19. *Journal of Transpersonal Psychology,* P.O. Box 4437, Stanford, California 94305.

CHAPTER 8

1. Harvey Cox, *The Seduction of the Spirit* (New York: Simon and Schuster, 1973); Martin E. Marty, *The Fire We Can Light* (New York: Doubleday and Company, 1973).